LOOKING AT LIFE THROUGH MY NEW BIFOCALS

Focusing on God's Purpose for the Second Half of Life

Jerry Brecheisen

wesleyan
publishing
house

Indianapolis, Indiana

Copyright © 2006 by Wesleyan Publishing House
Published by Wesleyan Publishing House
Indianapolis, Indiana 46250
Printed in the United States of America

ISBN-13: 978-0-89827-334-2
ISBN-10: 0-89827-334-x

INTRODUCTION

● ● ● ● ● ● ● ● ● ● ● ● ● ● ● ● ● ●

My first pair of bifocals was like my first bicycle. Both left me unsteady and not quite sure where I was going until I got there! So, the new bifocals weren't as traumatic. That is, until I tried to read the words on my computer monitor.

The folks at "Glasses in One Hour or More" promised the lenses would be perfect. I doubted it when the "technician," who made the glasses fit my face by just pushing on them, seemed to be wearing her glasses upside down. I soon realized that it was the new style. I guess when you wear glasses; it's supposed to look like you aren't wearing glasses.

In less than an hour after I left the "One Hour or More" store, I realized that the young lady's idea of perfect lenses didn't match my expectations about reading—or about seeing things at the end of my fingers. Trying to read the little words on the screen, I began to tip my head up and down like a bobble-head doll with a worn head-spring.

I tried everything. Moving the glasses down my nose. Moving the glasses up my nose. Tipping my chair. Rotating my head. Moving forward. Moving backward. Nothing worked. I finally found a solution: I took them off. The monitor screen looked like a London fog, but at least my neck muscles were getting a needed rest.

Bifocals are just part of the equipment for major leaguers playing in the second half of life; players, by the way, who were in God's Hall of Fame even before they retired. The rookies just don't have any idea of what life in the big leagues is all about! They don't understand that there'll be more strikeouts than walks, more trades than triumphs, and more sitting on the bench than playing. We know. And we know that the champions will be those who will live and learn—and learn to live at the same time.

I invite you to walk with me through the "wonder years"— the years of wondering where you put your glasses and wondering how you'll ever get the childproof caps off the medicine bottle. We'll share the ups and downs of life past the 50-mile marker. We'll have a few laughs, and we'll have times of sitting by the warm glow of God's Word. Hopefully, before we reach the last bend, we'll understand the abiding sense of worth God has for us.

You and I aren't just Social Security numbers. We are persons whom God loved enough, and trusted enough, to be given the toughest assignments in the most vulnerable of our years. We're not just here to keep the pharmacist's children in college. We're here to minister to the misery of others. We're here to bring hope to the worried, and we're here to show the folks that follow us how to live a good and godly life.

So, go ahead and give life a big bear hug. Embrace it. Let the whole world know what God can do through a life that is totally focused on Him—even when the bifocals need adjusting.

—JERRY BRECHEISEN

BUG BREATH

ugs everywhere can breathe a sigh of relief. Why? Science has declared that they can! Using powerful X-ray equipment, scientists have documented that bugs inhale and exhale. This is a great breakthrough, especially for the bugs. Up to this point, it was believed that air moved through tiny vents in their little bodies. Now it's known that bugs have teeny, little lungs. The X-rays show the rise and fall of bug abdomens, as if they were panting. I'm not a scientist, but from that description, I imagine the subjects of the study were middle-aged bugs that had just finished tying their shoes.

This breathing thing is good news for bugs. They probably all had a big party and threw all their little oxygen tanks into a tiny bonfire (the fireflies were probably in charge of the event). It's good news for me too. It shows that God is as good a caretaker as He is a creator. He wouldn't give those Lilliputians life without accompanying breath. He had it all worked out, even before the entomologists put a little mirror in front of a gnat's mouth to see if there was any moisture on it.

And doesn't it figure that you are the subject of greater care than a katydid? If God would put breath in them, just think how He will enable you to catch your breath in this breathtaking age! Imagine the great purposes for which He created you. All the sleep-aids in the world are no substitute for the fact of God's watchful care over your life.

Extra Point
When I am tired and can't fall asleep, I'll remember that my strength comes from the Lord.

"I am like an olive tree flourishing in the house of God;
I trust in God's unfailing love for ever and ever."
—Psalm 52:8

HOME VIDEOS

ideotaping usually has a downside. The tape-ees usually act way too silly for people of their age, national origin, or political persuasion. In an unplanned instant, we're left with a permanent record of men who inadvertently wore checkered shirts and striped pants and whose hair looks like it had been styled by Chubby Checker during a Twist demonstration in the '50s. Home videos have an even crueler side. Those who have recently lost weight by eating cucumber peelings are electronically transported back to their Wonder Bread years.

News videos are worse than the homemade kind. A whole nation watched as video feeds took it to the front lines of the Iraq War; or to airport terminals, where returning soldiers were welcomed by those who had been longing for the moment.

One among those bravehearts who didn't return was Army Specialist James Kiehl. He was among the soldiers of the 507th Maintenance Company from Fort Bliss, Texas, who gave their lives for their country. His parent's only comfort was the sight of a baptismal service that was videotaped in an Iraqi desert and played on the evening news. Before he went into battle, their son had joined the Army of Christ, and the videotaped baptism chronicled the swearing in ceremony.

But what those high tech cameras couldn't capture is this: A short while after his baptism, James was welcomed to the shores of eternity with the cheers of countless veterans of the Cross who had put their trust in one who had promised an eternal homecoming and found Him true. Army Specialist James Kiehl took his first heavenly steps holding the hand of the Master, whose smile lights the dawn and whose heart has enough welcomes for every weary soldier.

The Scriptures remind us that the Christ took the stinger out of the bee of death. The hurt is for awhile but the healing is forever.

Extra Point
In spite of the battle, I will focus on the homecoming.

"You welcomed him with rich blessings and placed
a crown of pure gold on his head."
—Psalm 21:3

GLUMPKIES

I f you've lived within a hundred-mile radius of Detroit, you've probably tasted a Glumpkie. I was in my twenties before I sampled one, during one of my favorite religious exercises: a church supper. "Glumpkie?" the volunteer server asked as she held out a large serving spoon with something that looked like it had been run over by a street sweeper. "Uh . . . Well . . . I guess," I replied with an obvious look of horror. "Glumpkies!" an elderly gentleman in line behind me interrupted. He was from the old country.

Since I was from the new country, I asked the man about Glumpkies. "Chopped meat," he started. "Add your onions, your garlic, your eggs, your rice, your crushed tomatoes . . . ." He suddenly stopped. He either was overcome with emotion or ran out of air during the recipe recitation. His much-younger wife continued demurely, "You roll all of the ingredients into cabbage leaves and cook them."

"How long?" I asked. I was still concerned about her husband, but I think she said, "Oh, about as long as it takes for survivor benefits to be verified by insurance underwriters."

Maybe you've been waiting in line for a benefit. Carrying the burden of a delinquent benefit is like wearing a fur with the animal still attached. Soon the smell detracts from the journey. Let's face it; these are days when entitlements are on the auction block. And the highest bidders shout from both sides of the congressional aisle.

If it makes you feel any better, Jesus didn't get all of His entitlements either. In fact, He willingly gave them up so that you and I could inherit the most important one: salvation. He had the entitlements of a king yet became a pauper. His throne was in the Temple of heaven, yet He lived homeless. He surrendered what He was owed to pay for our greatest debt.

Extra Point
Today, I will rejoice in the greatest benefit: my salvation.

"For the LORD watches over the way of the righteous, but the way of the wicked will perish."
—Psalm 1:6

NO-COUNTS

eing able to sing, dance, or balance steak knives tip down on the top of your head seems to fill an embarrassing void in the modern imagination, seeing that almost every TV station has its own talent show. One future-star program is even devoted to finding the most talented dogs! Great! Now, humans can be compared to a Cocker Spaniel that can whistle "Claire De Lune" through its nose while it sleeps.

"That no-count" is an expression that slips from the snarled lips of one who has given a low-performance score to another, perceiving them as having the ability or sociability of an earth mover with a dead battery.

It seems there is a bright future for no-counts, though. I read of a lady, who in looking for a new job, placed a classified ad and listed her qualifications as being anti-social, uncreative, and untalented. It worked! The phone rang off the hook, and she got a job—and a raise in pay!

Let's face it; our peak abilities often decline as our chronological age climbs. Even our friends of longstanding begin to kid us about what we can or cannot do. But a bright future still exists for us. In fact, we may be given a low score by every earthly judge and still come in first by the only evaluation that matters. God has already declared you a winner—even though He saw your miscues in advance. What you can or cannot do, or what you have done, has no bearing on what He already perceives you to be: His perfect creation.

The psalmist David was once declared a no-count by a table full of smug judges. Eliminated and alone in the long shadows of his sin, he wept over his failure and his future. But during his midnight hours, a Friend and Redeemer moved the coalition forces of mercy and grace into his backyard. By dawn, a sorry no-count was freed—and counted in the ranks of the righteous.

Extra Point
Today, I will let God pronounce His final
judgment on my abilities.

"They remembered that God was their Rock, that God
Most High was their Redeemer."
—Psalm 78:35

SAVE THE CHICKENS

'm always intrigued by well-intentioned groups that get their feathers ruffled by the fact that animals are in the food pyramid. One group even took on the dearly departed Colonel Sanders. They didn't like the way his company prepared chickens for human consumption. It's been awhile since the fowl fiasco, but it seemed to me that the do-gooders (who probably held secret meetings at a steakhouse) wanted the chickens to die of old age rather than the usual way.

Yes, Jesus cares about chickens, but He cares about people even more. When my granddaughter Lauren was three, she once stopped my writing by climbing into my lap. Standing up on my legs, she said: "Papa, I wish I was a bird." She giggled, as she flapped the little arms that previously encompassed my neck. "I would fly way up in the air, and Jesus would be right with me." Then she lectured me with a serious look and a pointed finger, "Jesus is always with us, you know."

I do know. Jesus said, "Look at the birds of the air; they do not sow or reap or store away in barns, and yet your heavenly Father feeds them. Are you not much more valuable than they?" (Matthew 6:26). I've had a few "sparrow days"—days when consuming insignificance smothered my duties and my dreams. Days when it seemed I'd lost my wings. Days when I felt as useful as a cement swimsuit. Yet on these days, the King of Glory chose to stop by unannounced, tiptoe to my chair, lay an unseen hand on my shoulder, and whisper over the chirping sounds of a hundred well-fed sparrows: "You are much more valuable than they."

I'm not the only one who has experienced "sparrow days." Look around. Next door. Across the street. In a nearby hospital. Even in the next room. There is someone who needs to know about God's care—through you. Someone who will feel the strength of God's hands through the strength He puts in yours. Someone who will hear the whispers of His Spirit through the song He sings through you. Every day offers an opportunity for you to say to someone, "You are valuable."

Extra Point
I will celebrate God's care for me today by
caring for someone else.

"I wash my hands in innocence, and go about your altar,
O LORD, proclaiming aloud your praise and
telling of all your wonderful deeds."
—Psalm 26:6–7

17

THE OLYMPIC "BLAMES"

• • • • • • • • • • • • • • • •

Every four years I pledge that I will not watch the summer Olympics. But my determination fades faster than the smoke from the fireworks of the opening ceremonies. It's not just the running, jumping, throwing, and rowing that gets my attention. It's the pre- and post-Olympic blames. The he-said-she-said-they-said of international officials and the haunting remorse of shoulda-coulda athletes.

Sooner or later some torchbearer or second-assistant, government Ya-hoo will take to the airwaves and give a bronze-medal tongue lashing to a judge, host country, or javelin thrower. The speech will have all the flair of a phonebook-reading. But words will fly like boyfriend names at a seventh-grade-girls' slumber party.

The official action off the field will be as exciting as the amateur action on the field. As sure as someone will trip over a hurdle, someone will complain about the lack of busses, the number of left-handed flag-bearers in the closing ceremonies, or the lukewarm chili on the official Olympics hot dogs. There will be more folks bent out of shape than at a school for contortionists. But the Games and "blames" will be back.

Speaking of blame, have you ever won a medal in your own Olympic "Blames"? Have you noticed that the closer you get to the finish line, the more often blames arise? You lack this, or want that. You would . . . if only! It may affect every area of your life: physical, emotional, and spiritual. You strive for a balance that will keep you out of the psych clinic and the joint replacement center.

Wellness isn't a new issue. The same Christ who "grew in wisdom and stature, and in favor with God and men" took the issues of incompleteness with Him to the cross.

God's grace is deeper and wider and higher than your long-ing to be whole. You do the leg work—the exercise, check-ups, and diet. He'll do the rest. He'll bring health to your inner person through His indwelt presence and power.

Extra Point
Today I will do the things that will make me stronger—
including relying on God.

"A cheerful look brings joy to the heart, and
good news gives health to the bones."
—Proverbs 15:30

DONUT DYNASTY

I was having my morning cup of coffee when I got the news: donut sales have been rising—at least for one company! It's been a long and bitter fight. In one corner, wearing a Lycra gym suit, a brave nutritionist tries to convince the public of the long term benefits of soy. In the other corner, wearing a comfort-fit jumpsuit, the brave traditionalist offers the public what it has always wanted: taste. Since this certain donut chain had just declared record sales, I celebrated with a trip to one of its shops to offer my congratulations—and stayed for the refreshments.

The pining souls who had been pretending that lettuce leaves and thimble-size portions of diet gelatin were more than filling had jumped over the police barriers—and a few policemen— to try a little filling of their own (namely jelly, cream, and chocolate). I'm happy for the donut. It has been as maligned as a new Mercedes with four of those temporary tires. (I think they call them "donut" tires!) And I'm happy that taste has reclaimed its rightful territory on the menus of life. It won't last long. Lurking in the culinary shadows is a mad scientist who will declare that global warming and the decline in the California condor population is due to the proliferation of fat grams.

Okay! So maybe a few lettuce leaves and a dish of diet gelatin might not be all bad. Maybe fitness is as much of a statement as donut sales. It certainly would help elevator inspectors worry less about capacity. And it might not be a bad idea to use the stationery bike for something other than a clothes rack.

But fitness for our gain rather than God's glory isn't worthy of the "temple." He does the final weigh-in.

Extra Point

Today, I will let the Word of God be the light for my path—including my diet and exercise.

"Do not be wise in your own eyes; fear the LORD and shun evil. This will bring health to your body and nourishment to your bones."
—Proverbs 3:7–8

FORGET SOMETHING?

ver get halfway through the day and remember that you forgot something? Your brain cells faint and fall to the floor of your cranium. You struggle for a keyword: Appointment? Call? Payment? Keys? And then you spend the rest of the day trying to make your mental ends meet.

I forgot something important. I'll give you a clue. It was an anniversary—a 215th anniversary! Now before you panic, hit the speed dial number for the florist, and rush to the "Buck-for-Everything" store, neither you nor I missed our wedding anniversaries. We missed the 215th anniversary of the U.S. Constitution.

So far, I've remembered not to forget my wedding anniversary. That's not to say it won't happen in the future. Each day past the halftime of life brings me new ways of forgetting things—like where I left my car or my checkbook.

Forgetting the anniversary of the Constitution doesn't take any work. If memory serves me (and it's not always that obedient), the last invitation to the anniversary was published prominently in the newspaper—near the last pages of the second section—in the advertising section, right next to the hail-damage-markdowned Chevys at *Cars-a-Million* and near the fifty-percent-off ad for "famous designer faux suede coats" (which means very few Suedes gave their lives for the garments). This is too bad. Brave souls put their lives on the same line with their signatures. Most gave everything they had so that we could enjoy what we have.

As we age, other things slip along with our memory. Muscles migrate. Hair sneaks off our head into the sink. Our eyesight plays peek-a-boo, and our teeth often need tiny steel support beams. Adjusting to changing body conditions is challenging. But one thing doesn't change: God's opinion of us. No matter where we are in the process of mental and physical maturity, we are still a perfect creation in the sight of our Creator.

Extra Point
I will look at myself through my heavenly Father's eyes.

"Your eyes saw my unformed body. All the days
ordained for me were written in your book
before one of them came to be."
—Psalm 139:16

JAWBONE SCIENCE

love it when scientists discover a human bone fragment and then proceed to tell us everything about the person. One bone! "Oh yes," science rubs its chin. "This was the Epidural Analgesic Zerogravitis man. He lived in a small village near the equator approximately ten million years ago. His name was Frank. He was the town council president, and his wife, Edith Ann, drove an earth-tone-colored wheel."

I struggle to link a 25-piece puzzle of the Statue of Liberty, so don't ask me for any expertise in bone fragmenting. Jawbone science isn't for beginners. I just hope they picked up the right bone. I could be the distant cousin of a prehistoric water buffalo. The only thing I know about ancient things is from a geology class in college. I collected enough rocks during that year to add a bypass on the Great Wall of China. Rocks everywhere. I ran out of Dixie cups, so I started piling them behind the sofa in the living room.

One day a friend came over to the house and sat in a chair across from the sofa. We were talking, and he must not have appreciated my opinion. He looked in my direction and exclaimed, "You've got rocks in your head!" I thought the pile must have outgrown the sofa. "Yes, I know," I said embarrassingly. "But I'm throwing them out at the end of the semester."

I'm amazed that so many experts can seemingly solve the past, and yet be so stymied about the present or future. I don't know a lot about archaeology. But I do know a little about theology; enough to believe that my present and future have already been cataloged. My age and my ages are in His hands—and His hands alone. Nothing will happen that has not first been approved. I am a victor, determined to focus more on where I'm going than where I am.

Extra Point
I will look at the appointments of life rather
than the accidents.

"Keep me as the apple of your eye; hide me in
the shadow of your wings."
—Psalm 17:8

THIRTY-THOUSAND-YEAR PAYOFF

. . . .

Next to cooking, math was always my worst subject in school. Forget cooking! I haven't even figured how to set the clock on the microwave after a power outage. So if you drop in unannounced, don't expect anything from me but Cheerios with skim milk and a dinner mint. Math is worse. I'm still learning my divisions. And thankfully, in all these years, no one has stopped me on the street and said, "Excuse me, sir, do you speak Algebra?"

On a trip to Rome, I nearly sold Alabama before I figured out the currency exchange. It's so bad that I've never tried to preach from the book of Numbers in the Bible. I was afraid there'd be an equation halfway through the verses I was trying to read out loud.

Living with a math deficit is challenging at best. So in a way, I could sympathize with the man who had embezzled millions from his associates. When the judge ordered him to pay it back, he announced that he'd spent it all. The judge ordered him to prison; and then told him he would have to make monthly payments on what he owed financially. That amounted to thirty bucks a month over thirty-thousand years! The poor crook probably needed a Friend of the Court just to help him carry the payment book to his car! Sometimes aging is like carrying a thirty-thousand-year payment book.

Funny thing about aging. Everybody experiences it, yet everyone takes cheap shots at it. Take a look at the stereo-type section of the card shop. The "Over the hill" products are as numerous as age spots on an octogenarian (Oops!). And the "getting older" cards have messages sharp enough to make Robert Schuler grumpy!

No one but you knows what you're capable of. So don't let the opinions of the under-aged make you dress like them, act like them, or feel guilty for not being them. Be the best "yourself" you can be. Take a lesson from nature, the older the tree, the tougher the bark. You may be a candle short of middle age, or a roman numeral shy of three-score-and-ten, but you still know the inestimable worth of you.

Extra Point
I refuse to act my age—or anyone else's age.

"They will still bear fruit in old age, they
will stay fresh and green."
—Psalm 92:14

THE 18-MINUTE GAP

hose old enough to remember when Elvis was an Army private and King at the same time might also remember when time stood still in Washington. There was an 18-minute gap in history when a White House secretary (inadvertently) stepped on the ERASE pedal of a dictation machine and sent the comments of President Richard Nixon into space. Most can barely remember what that infamous absence of candor was all about. Frankly, I'm at an age when remembering where I put my reading glasses is an effort. But if my long-term recollection serves me, the "sentences in absentia" probably dealt with some uninvited guests at a Washington Hotel who had tried to get into the office suite of the Democrats in the worst possible way. Eighteen minutes of Watergate history had been forever lost.

As a public speaker, I've had my share of 18-minute gaps. Somewhere between the introduction and conclusion, my mind hit the ERASE button. Once I was giving an illustration about influence by suggesting how the fragrance of a rose permeates a sealed glass jar. Making the contrast, I then tried to illustrate how the fragrance of a dill pickle would make a negative influence. "There's one thing you could say about a dill pickle . . . ," I started. Then time stood still!

I couldn't think of anything to say about a dill pickle. Nothing! I couldn't even remember what color they were.

I quickly left the produce section and resumed the lesson on influence. Time stood still but eventually truth marched on. It was the same during Watergate. The exploits of a few soldiers of misfortune affected the entire political process. But as a result, character took to the platform and spoke louder than a thousand candidates.

Character still speaks. It speaks of doing right no matter the consequences. Of living as if our lives held no higher meaning than serving our Creator and His creation. Of learning to love, daring to plan, and reaching out to hold the hand of God, even when we can't see Him.

Extra Point

Today, I will make my character count for something— and for someone.

"Teach me your way, O LORD, and I will
walk in your truth; give me an undivided
heart, that I may fear your name."
—Psalm 86:11

BACKYARD GARDEN

● ● ● ● ● ● ● ● ● ● ● ● ● ● ● ● ●

My wife was raised on a small farm in the thumb of Michigan. She walked only feet or a few yards to take her pick of fresh tomatoes, carrots, green beans, or sweet corn. The son of gospel-singing parents, I was raised in a travel trailer. The nearest fruits and vegetables were in a truck stop or a neighborhood restaurant that sold plates of grease disguised as "Daily Specials."

In the interest of marital harmony I agreed to help my wife plant a garden. The thoughts of her re-living life on the farm, and visions of fresh sweet corn sitting on a dinner table, drove me beyond my skill level. "I just want a tiny garden," the missus said. I thought she meant a galvanized tub on the patio filled with potting soil, decorated with seed packets on Popsicle sticks. She was actually thinking about digging up dirt in the backyard! I barely learned to drive a car, so starting and steering a garden tiller was as challenging as convincing a rhinoceros to model a two-piece swimsuit.

After nearly tearing a rotator cuff tugging on the start cord, dislocating a family of azaleas, and hearing neighbors calling their children indoors, I finally got the four-by-six-foot burial plot for seedlings ready for the ceremony. "I'll handle the planting," my anxious wife said, handing me a cool drink of water and a Valium. I let her. She was a master, putting seeds in straight rows, adding the right amount of fertilizer, covering the future veggies with soil as if she were adjusting the covers over a newborn.

Soon after I put the snow shovels in the garage (which doesn't necessarily coincide with the first days of spring), and thanks to my skill with the tiller, the wealth of buried vegetable treasures blossomed.

God has given us a garden of wealth: His eternal Word. Even when you're tired, a daily dig through its soil will invigorate your soul enough to give your body an edge for the day.

Extra Point
Today I will dig a little deeper into the soil of the
Scriptures.

"I rejoice in following your statutes as
one rejoices in great riches."
—Psalm 119:14

REAL PRIESTS

For three long and rewarding years, I served as a volunteer chaplain for a city fire department. With over 100 firefighters and their families in my charge, a full-time job as the pastor of a growing church, a TV ministry, and a wife and two daughters to care for, I often felt as stressed as a wing counter on a bee farm. Riding fire trucks and working fires was the fun part. The downside was answering calls in the middle of the night and wearing the previous chaplain's turnout gear. The white helmet and coat had "Father DeMott" printed in bright gold letters on them. DeMott was a Roman Catholic priest who had been the department chaplain for several years. Despite trying to explain that I was a protestant minister and not a Catholic priest, I was called "Father" for the entire tour of duty. I felt like saying, "I'm not a real priest, I just play one on TV."

In our spiritual life, we need a real priest. A high priest. One who is blameless. One who is exalted enough to be our Lord and yet common enough to be our brother. One who isn't afraid of our storms. Who'll journey with us even when everyone else has taken the exit ramp. Who'll talk to us and for us, rather than about us.

The New Testament writer had found one in the person of the Christ who sits on the throne of eternity in the company of angels, and yet spends the ages whispering our concerns into the ear of the Father. "Because Jesus lives forever, he has a permanent priesthood" (Hebrews 7:24).

Sounds like a good job for His children as well! Whispering the cares of a friend, family member, or associate into the listening ear of the Heavenly Father. Of course He already knows about them. But He has determined that our telling helps our growing.

Extra Point
I will talk with God about someone's needs today.

"I call on you, O God, for you will answer me;
give ear to me and hear my prayer."
—Psalm 17:6

"YOU CAN'T MISS IT!"

The most dangerous phrase in the English language: "You can't miss it." I know because I am a card-carrying member of the Missed It club. I was inducted during a trip to Pennsylvania. The interior of Pennsylvania. The outback. The area Lewis and Clark had circled on their map when they found Montana.

Luckily, in my wandering quest to find the place where I was to speak that evening, I happened on a convenience store. A small store, standing like a half-burned candle in a typhoon. The lonely cashier was overjoyed when I walked through the door. "May I help you—please," she said with polite pathos. I said, "I'm looking for a church." She replied, "Oh, have you tried mine? We have a new pastor. He's only 20, but he preaches like he was 70. 'Has eight kids, and one in the oven. He's preaching a series on the fruits of the Spirit. This week's about self-control."

I interrupted. "No ma'am, I already have a church. I'm trying to find the church where I am to speak." She looked sad, "Won't they let you speak at your church?" It was like a train wreck in process, but I finally convinced her that I needed directions. I should have known. In the "outback" of Pennsylvania, you look for landmarks. She began, and didn't stop. "You go a quarter mile to the Yoders', turn left at that big rock by the fence, keep going another . . . oh, 'bout a mile, maybe. You'll pass a brown cow standing under a tree, and then bear right at the crossroad. Down that road—I don't know its name, it's a number or somethin'— keep going for about a half-hour. You can't miss it." I did.

We live in a world of global positioning satellites and talking maps. But often we miss the way. God has given you detailed instructions for your daily spiritual journey. There are landmarks in His Word that will get you where you need to go. You can walk with a sturdy confidence along the roads of time to the shores of eternity.

Extra Point
Where will I trust God to take me today?

"It is not good to have zeal without knowledge,
nor to be hasty and miss the way."
—Proverbs 19:2

THE GOOD WORM

● ● ● ● ● ● ● ● ● ● ● ● ● ● ● ● ● ● ●

I remember when one of the highest forms of technology was the Etch-a-Sketch. Marvelous invention! No hard drive crashes. No memory upgrades. No night classes to learn how to find the ON button. You simply had to turn a couple of white dials and maneuver tiny rivers of magnesium into the semblance of a horse or something. When you made a mistake, you didn't worry about finding the DELETE button without your reading glasses. You just gripped the red plastic monitor by its sides, held it above your head, and shook away all the evidence.

I also remember when worms were most often associated with either fishing or Fido. Now computers have worms— viruses that make computers sick, and make you sick of computers! They're bad worms; electronic undercover agents that slither past your virus protection software and turn the files on your hard drive into oatmeal.

One "glitch geek" came up with a "good worm." It supposedly searched for "bad worms" and deleted infected files. But the "good worm" wasn't that good. It supposedly put speed bumps in the path of data flowing in and out of your computer. I guess! My insight on the technology

36

wouldn't be enough to make a contact for the left iris of a katydid.

I do know about bad worms, though. I know that I was born with a flaw handed down by my great-fore-parent, Adam. I know that his disobedience against the will and Word of God left me vulnerable to attacks of far greater significance than those launched against computers. I know that it inched unsuspected into my life—even when I was going about doing good—and caused a spiritual crash.

And I also know about a good worm—a really good worm. Willingly, I gave the good worm of grace an invitation to invade the hard drive of my heart and delete the files of sin. And the path of blessing that followed has never been erased.

Extra Point
Today, I will release the "good worm of grace."

"But I trust in your unfailing love;
my heart rejoices in your salvation."
—Psalm 13:5

AUCTION HOUSE

· · · · · · · · · · · · · · · · · · · ·

I love auctions. The atmosphere. The participants. The auctioneers. The accumulated stuff. It's a wonderful way to spend a Saturday morning. Folks my age like the process. First, they like the company. Their driveways will never have as many cars in it. Second, they like to see folks pay cash for junk that's been accumulating in their attics, basements, and garages. Third, they like to see perfectly sensible people try to get the attention of the auctioneer — who is usually so hyper he could be a poster child for caffeine addiction. They casually wave a tiny sign, pull at their ears, rub their noses, raise their eyebrows, or just plain holler.

Fierce bidding often breaks out. Someone gets their eye on a quilt that looks like it might have covered the lap of Betsy Ross as she sewed stars onto the American Flag. Little do they know that Aunt Sally knitted the quilt from Uncle Ted's stained T-shirts two Christmases ago, and it's been stored on a nail in the rafters of the attic ever since. The howling for the items often rises to the level of a church business meeting over the construction of a crows nest above the pipe organ to house a new drum set.

For me, the thought of investing hard-earned cash on the

promise of a purchase is a bit of a stretch. Besides, why should I bid on the future when I can get it for free! God has not only revealed the future in His installment of 66 books (the Bible), He has already revealed the ending to the series. And guess what? We win! Time doesn't. The economy doesn't. Evil doesn't. Pain doesn't. Loneliness doesn't. We do—we who march in the parade that has an old rugged Cross at the front.

Extra Point
In spite of occasional losses, I will focus on
the promise of my final victory.

"With God we will gain the victory, and he will
trample down our enemies."
—Psalm 60:12

THE CHEAP SEATS

he seating at professional basketball games comes in four varieties: courtside, luxury suite, regular, and "Here, take these binoculars with you." I once opted for the binocular section. In the old days, before it was politically incorrect to refer to noses, it was called the nosebleed section.

By the time I climbed to my assigned seat (which still cost more than my childhood appendectomy) I was nearly unconscious from altitude sickness and hypothermia. There was a vendor in the aisle. "Popcorn . . . hot dogs . . . coffee . . . long underwear?" he droned. I wasn't paying that much attention. I was busy giving my dying wishes to a friend. "Bob, in case I don't make it, be sure my wife doesn't sell my Johnny Cash tour bus replica on eBay."

Moments before tip-off, I celebrated making it to the summit. Planting a flag in the drink holder, I sang, "Thro many dangers toils and snares, I have already come . . . ," and sat down in a seat that was designed by Twiggy's weight loss instructor. Suddenly I noticed that I was sitting behind a fan wearing an oversized, foam-rubber replica of a ten-gallon hat. For the rest of the game, the only time I got to see the tiny "ants" on the basketball court throw dust specks at one another was when "Annie Oakley" leaned down to pick up her dropped popcorn.

For every child of God there is a promised trip to the summit. There won't be any cheap seats in heaven, though. Even the oversized throne in the center will reflect matchless glory and splendor. And the grandstands will be filled with multitudes of mercy-folk, who can only reminisce about the good times, while angel choirs sing their "Hallelujahs!" into overtime. So why should we worry about the seating sections of earth, when we really ought to be thinking about the luxury suites of eternity?

Extra Point
Today I will spend more time worrying about the luxury suites of heaven than the cheap seats of earth.

"Trust in the LORD with all your heart and lean not on your own understanding; in all your ways acknowledge him, and he will make your paths straight."
—Proverbs 3:5–6

THREE-SIXTEENED

. . . .

"How tall are you?" the nurse asked as I stood on the scales during a recent physical. I think she was trying to reconcile the height-weight difference. I'll admit it; I've been short all of my life. I was born short, and I've been trying to measure up to the tall folks ever since. I nearly caught up when I was in my thirties, thanks to a pair of cowboy boots I bought at an outlet store on the way to Florida. But now that I've reached the "middle ages," even boots leave me looking up. I'm losing ground (or should I say, I'm seeing more of it!). I'm shrinking. "I shortened those slacks," the missus said recently. "And they look like they need to be shortened again." She's right. Time plays a cruel hoax on those of us with vertical deficits: the longer we live, the shorter we get. At this pace, by the time I'm in my eighties I'll need a stepladder to reach the top of a sidewalk curb. I'm really not as concerned as I was in my twenties, though. When you're middle-aged, height is only a numbers game.

For many years, numbers have cast a lengthening shadow over us. Nine-eleven has become our historical Point of reference—a fence line between the relatively calm past and the potentially chaotic future. To me, there are other numerical combinations that are even more important: three-sixteen, for example. John 3:16. Simply put, since the day I was three-sixteened—since the day I applied God's master plan of salvation to my seeking heart—my nine-elevens have been more manageable. No, my life hasn't been free from personal disasters. I haven't been immune to disease or distress. But when I was three-sixteened I gained a confidence that is anchored in the One and Only.

You may be as nervous as a purebred poodle walking through a car wash. But your nine-elevens don't have to "deep-six" your life. Go ahead; trust Him with the *pre-* and *post-* of your journey. And remember: what's *four*-given is *four*-gotten.

Extra Point
I will face the present and the future with confidence
in the One who has been in both!

"For the sake of your name, O LORD,
forgive my iniquity, though it is great."
—Psalm 25:11

PERFECT TAPS

M y heart goes out to anyone playing brass in front of a crowd. I used to play a trumpet. Used to! One of my last public performances was during my impressionable adolescence—the age when a cowlick or a zit can be as disastrous as a NASCAR driver making U-turns during a race. The auditorium was open-sided, hot, and humid. Lightning flashes were threatening the power of our 25-watt sound system. And then it happened. I broke the brass instrument rule of rules.

They were taking up the offering in Kentucky Fried Chicken buckets; I was standing center stage with trumpet in hand, and enough Brylcreem in my hair to slick the runway of an aircraft carrier. I blew the first note—and immediately finished my performance. I walked over to the edge of the platform and pried chewing gum out of the mouthpiece of my trumpet, while Dad finished the song with a piano solo.

Imagine my distress to learn that because of a shortage of buglers, electronic taps-playing is getting to be the norm. For future bugle-ists, whether a veteran smartly clad in a military uniform or a junior higher trying to see over the collar of a borrowed band outfit, the news is brighter than the smile of an orthodontist's daughter in her high school graduation picture. Thanks to some electronic gizmo, buglers can play perfect "Taps"—the musical strains that honor our bravest and best at their memorial. The "musician" simply puts the horn to his or her lips and pretends to play, while the sound tech pushes a button that sends the digitally produced song wafting through the air.

Wouldn't it be great to have some kind of perfection living inside us that would turn our discord into delight! There is. A life yielded to and empowered by the Holy Spirit is always playing heaven's tune—no matter how battered the instrument or how ill-fitting the uniform.

Extra Point
I will yield my imperfection to God's perfection.

"Create in me a pure heart, O God, and renew
a steadfast spirit within me."
—Psalm 51:10

MENDING BROKEN HEARTS

● ● ● ● ● ● ● ● ● ● ● ● ● ● ● ●

The news grabbed me like a new grandma at a family reunion with a wallet full of baby pictures. Medical researchers had theorized that heart muscle damage could be reversed—hearts could be mended. By injecting a certain chemical, once-tepid tickers would run like a Timex on Mountain Dew. They think heart muscle cells can be revived after an attack, like one brought on by the news that Donald Trump is getting a buzz cut.

So head for the cafeteria and let the wonderful folks in blue uniforms, white shoes, and brown hair nets portion you out a grandma-slice of rhubarb pie to go with your daily special. If your blood vessels shut down, you could be a candidate for new heart cells. You might want to consider one thing, however: The testing has been limited (which gives a swing vote to the asparagus salad).

I've had a broken heart. Once I went to pick up a high school date and she came sauntering down the front steps on the arm of a friend! Crash! The minute I saw them, I knew my relationship with the perky brunette was in more trouble than a peroxide blond in a pool of chlorine. And I knew the next time I heard Pat Boone sing "Love Letters in the Sand," I'd be thinking of high tide washing away the remnants of my romance with dead fish and seaweed.

There's a lot of heartbroken-ness going around these days. And not all of it comes from grandma-portions of rhubarb pie or stolen dates. Some of it comes from people simply trying to get on with life. Who knew there'd be a speed bump just around that unexpected curve in the road? God did.

And He not only expresses His provision and care in person, He appoints ambassadors like you and me to go to the places where people are hurting and provide help. Christ modeled compassion for the needy and gave all of us the commission to follow His path.

Extra Point
I will honor Christ by ministering to the needs
of those around me.

"He who despises his neighbor sins, but blessed
is he who is kind to the needy."
—Proverbs 14:21

A FOUR-LEGGED FOE

rixie was the name of our first dog. She was a registered fox terrier with the wit of Mark Twain, the loyalty of Winston Churchill, and the nerves of Don Knotts. I was her personal trainer. I taught her to shake hands, pray, sit, lie down, roll over, and fetch a tennis ball. In return, she taught me how to feed her dog biscuits and clean up pet residue. Her love was genuine, her excitement contagious, and her manners acclaimed. If she would have run for congress, I would have given her my vote.

Imagine my surprise to learn that a dog actually did run for congress; a write-in candidate for the house of representative primary race in one state. I thought of Trixie. She could have shaken voter hands, fetched checks, licked the hands of babies, gathered more applause than an absent-minded philanthropist at a fund raising dinner, and prayed over the election outcome. The actual canine candidate had an uphill struggle. First was the problem of pulling the lever in the voting booth. Second was the campaign funding. Its opponent probably had a war chest of millions. The Fido write-in probably had to forage through Hefty bags at the curbside. But rather than taking such a quasi-collie campaign too lightly, let us be reminded that candidates with equal or less qualifications have been named Top Dog in times past!

You may not have to fetch checks or forage through curb-side culinary delights to make an impression. You may simply utilize the skills that were factory installed in your heart and life. In fact use your skills in ministry to others. For instance, the prayer regimen you have learned in the heat of life's battle may be just the warmth a cold heart needs to understand God's love and forgiveness. The treasures of God's Word that you have discovered in your own study may be just the riches needed by another. What God gives, He wants us to share.

Extra Point
I will look for ways to utilize the ministry skills
that God has given to me.

"The righteous care about justice for the poor,
but the wicked have no such concern."
—Proverbs 29:7

ARTIFICIAL INTELLIGENCE

● ● ● ● ● ● ● ● ● ● ● ● ● ● ● ● ●

Computers are a wonderful invention. For mere hundreds of dollars you can take the on ramp to the information expressway, automatically figure your income tax, and download more jingles, jokes, and Jello pudding recipes than you could use in a lifetime. That is, when computer works. When it doesn't, you'll either have to call a computer technician or your youngest grandchild. That's what I do. And both responders make me feel dumber than a brick with a gravel deficit.

One research team is even scanning facial expressions so that our computers will get to know us better. By entering the data into the artificial mind that runs our computer, it will learn to be human (which is still on the "do-list" of many humans themselves). It's just a step behind robots in the home and at the office. For office managers, firing folks won't be as difficult. If a robot refuses to take a CPR course, you could simply pull its plug.

Personally, I don't think we need artificial intelligence. We simply need to be smart enough to realize that we're not as wise as God. And He alone knows the *limits of our limits*.

Conversely, He knows the things we have the ability to do—things that express our uniqueness.

For example, if everyone played the piano, there wouldn't be an audience. Someone has to be gifted in listening. Finding what you're able to do well enough to bring hope, help, or healing to another is a real find! You don't need a hundred spiritual gifts tests. One will do. In fact, if you're as nervous about taking tests as I am, you can just play it by ear. Start with what you can do. If someone wasn't gifted to change a tire, the world really would be flat! And if another didn't have the ability to see beyond the barriers, buildings and ministries and organizations would only be needs on tomorrow's horizon.

Extra Point
I will find and use my gifts to the fullest
extent of God's help.

"Do not withhold good from those who deserve it, when it
is in your power to act."
—Proverbs 3:27

SUPER BOWLS
AND SUPERSIZE

● ● ● ● ● ● ● ● ● ● ● ● ● ● ● ● ● ● ●

ach year, before spring shines and winter fades, marketing mavens take their corporate credit cards to the limit by sponsoring stupid commercials during halftime of the Super Bowl. Millions of dollars will be spent on capturing the attention of folks who have probably left the room to grab another slice of pizza or refill the salsa bowl. Some will watch out of curiosity, however, as a hundred *what's-its* are touted by as many *who's-its* in 15, 30, or 60-second intervals. Well-known entertainers will sing and dance for the "live" audience in the stadium. Some of the entertainers will be talented; others will make it obvious they should have kept their day jobs.

The rest of the manufacturing food chain has scooped up the "Super" concept like a fumbled football and ran with it all the way to the end zone. You can't walk the slippery floors of a fast food restaurant without being offered to supersize your fries and drink. Most fast food chains expand their profits this way. During a recent shopping trip for casual slacks, I learned that these restaurants are expanding more than just profits. I started in the "trim" section and sadly worked my way through the "regulars" and "extra regulars" to the "expand-o-waist" bin after making frequent trips to the fitting room where louvered half-doors covered me only from stooped shoulders to knobby knees. Before the pants were even in the bag, I realized that these marketing folks had not only increased their bottom-line, they had supersized my waistline!

Jesus taught that less is enough. Tiny mustard seeds grow. A few loaves and fishes feed thousands. A small step of faith by man turns to a giant leap of mercy for mankind. Why? It's the Jesus factor. You see, if He was all that you had, you would have more than enough. His supersizing works on the inside, creating a place where peace overshadows earthly profits, where comfort soothes earthly pain and eternal glory contrasts worldly pleasures.

Extra Point
Today, I will practice being content with who I am and what I have, instead of buying the lie that I always need something more.

"He covers the sky with clouds; he supplies the earth with rain and makes grass grow on the hills."
—Psalm 147:8

LIVE BY FAITH

. . . .

L iving in the Middle Ages—while you're social security is up for bids like a heifer in an auction barn, and you're only one broken femur away from having your health insurance revoked—is risky business. Purposefully living on the edge makes as much sense as requesting the "No Novocain" section when getting a root canal at a dental school. But some folks seem to be up for it.

I watched a TV show called "Fear Factor" the other night. I was taking a walk to nowhere on my treadmill and trying to get my mind off the exercise part of the trip. In a quest for fifty-thousand-dollars, contestants lined up with smiles on their faces and sweat on their palms to alternately hold their breath under water 'til they turned purple, eat a plate full of fish bait, and jump off a tall building while tied to bungee cords the length of suspenders on a second-grader. Sounds like a lot of fun, right? I caught the last segment. Three finalists—who would probably spend their winnings on plastic surgery to remove the scars—drove a speeding car up the lowered wheel ramps of a moving auto-truck carrier, put on the brakes, and parked suddenly behind a used Plymouth. It reminded me of my driver's education class.

Most of us are in a "fear factor" situation. We're smiling while our palms are sweating. We're going too fast for our age, and if we're not careful, we'll end up crashing into someone who is standing still! Our survival to the finish line isn't based on what we can bear. It's based on what the Christ of Calvary has already borne. Risk taking is okay as long as it stays within God-given parameters. We conquer fear in the confidence and courage of one who suffered the worst so that He could give us His very best. We can trust Him when we can't trust *anyone* or *anything* else.

Extra Point
Today, I will let God be greater than my greatest fear.

"I will lie down and sleep in peace, for you alone,
O LORD, make me dwell in safety."
—Psalm 4:8

WORD GAMES

. . . .

t finally happened. One-hundred channels on the TV and I ran out of things to watch. *I'll turn to the learning channel*, I thought. The very words suggested that something worthwhile might be on that channel. Don't tell this to a living soul! But for the next hour, I watched the finals of a Scrabble® championship! It was a 'tween season: 'tween football and NASCAR. So it was the nearest thing to sports I could find.

The action was fast and furious. Competitors reached into a **black** bag filled with letter or blank tiles, pulled them out **quicker** than a silver polisher at a jeweler's convention, and put them on their tile holders. Even before their turn to put the letters on the board for a double-this, triple-that, they were arranging their letter tiles into words. I was amazed at their quick minds, but I missed the sports things. There weren't any time-outs. No trips to the board by trainers with water bottles. No sponsor logos on their shirts. No pit stops for a change of eyeglasses. No spectators with their faces or stomachs painted with team colors. Probably the only hazards to the game are carpal-tunnel syndrome, strained egos, or brain freeze.

There was a color commentator for the Word Games! Talking softly into a microphone as if Tiger Woods was ready to make a tournament-winning putt, the commentator said something like, "Frank is referring to his official Scrabble® dictionary. Let's see what word he can make from two X's, three Y's, and a Z."

Some reference books are for everyone, though. The Bible is one. It contains nothing new, but it's always fresh. It is often unpopular, but it's always powerful. In fact, in just three words its author won the championship with a triple-word bonus: "It is finished" (John 19:30).

Those in Calvary's cheap seats thought they had heard a surrender. How silly! It was the lyrics to a love song, sung by heaven over the battlefields of despair. And it put a melody in the hearts of people who thought their hopes had been nailed to a tree.

Extra Point
I will realize that God-blessed endings have
God-filled beginnings.

"For this God is our God for ever and ever; he will be our
guide even to the end."
—Psalm 48:14

NINETEEN-HUNDRED-YEAR SADNESS

• • • • • • • • • • • • • • • • • •

The Jewish community observes *Tisha B'ava*. With a 24-hour fast, Hebrew faithful mark the nineteen-hundred-and-thirty-second anniversary of the AD 70 destruction of the Jewish Temple in Jerusalem by the Romans. A Rabbi described the observance, "It is a day of mourning and reflection. We gather in dimly lit synagogues to read the Book of Lamentations."

I would be the last to make light of the deep feelings that accompany such a meeting. And I would be the first to appreciate a religious culture that has as much of a handle on its past as it does on its present or future. But I couldn't help thinking about that meeting. "We gather in dimly lit synagogues to read the book of Lamentations."

Frankly, I've been in meetings like that—and they weren't in a Jewish synagogue! Akin to pep rallies at the college of mortuary science, some were church business meetings. At times they were opening exercises of Sunday school, when sleepy people gathered to sing rousing renditions of "Rock of Ages" and give away embossed pencils. Others were college chapel services, on the occasions when someone like the history professor spoke on the significance of the Ming Dynasty in the worship styles of the modern church.

Maybe you've gone to a "mourning" worship service when you were the only one in attendance, reflecting on some bad things that have happened to you. Perhaps they didn't happen 1900 years ago. Perhaps they happened nineteen years or nineteen hours ago. The world sneaked up behind you and gave you a Karate chop on your arthritic shoulder. A word. A deed. A failed promise. A sudden sickness. It caught you by surprise and left you with a lingering bruise.

How long will it last? As long as you let it. Obviously, the possibilities range from nineteen seconds to nineteen hundred years. Paul, the apostle, went for the former (Philippians 3:13–14). He checked the baggage of his sorrows at the ticket counter for his flight to heaven. And the good news: God lost Paul's luggage!

Extra Point

I will check the luggage of my past and just
enjoy the journey.

"But with you there is forgiveness;
therefore you are feared."
—Psalm 130:4

IDENTITY THEFT

I love being a grandparent. I love watching our children take pride over their own child's sit-ups and spit-ups. I also like the perks. I like going first in line at family gatherings. I like the discounts in the "Over 50" column on the restaurant menu. And I like holding the newest grandchild in the family portrait—and then handing it over to its parents when it gets fussy. Grandparents even have their own language. After the first grandchild is born they began to talk like they have a mouth full of jalapeño peppers and the mind of a two-year-old. "Ewe, you cutie wittle wover. Ewe wook sooo much wike your mommie-pie did when she was a wittle, wittle guurl." *Who's-got-you* is a one-word phrase uttered in either a low pitched or high pitched voice by grandparents when they temporarily surrender their grandchild to the arms of another.

There'll be times when you'll wonder whose you are. Your used-to-be's have been replaced with your are-now's. And change is always a bit unsettling—socially, economically, and physically. It may even affect your thinking. Your once-pleasant disposition has been clouded by lingering backaches. And there are times when you feel as out of place as a Tibetan monk at a hairpiece convention.

The Apostle Paul gave us an inspired and eternal assurance. He said, "If we live, we live to the Lord; and if we die, we die to the Lord" (Romans 14:8). Nothing could steal his belongings. Through faith in the Lord Jesus Christ, the apostle had a place card at God's family table that wouldn't be blown off by the winds of his time.

So do you! God has a place for you at His reserved table. Wherever you go, whomever you meet, and whatever happens, you represent the corporation of the Kingdom as an heir to the Chairman of the Board. Don't forget *who's-got-you*.

Extra Point
Today I will rejoice in my place at God's reserved table.

"Though my father and mother forsake me,
the LORD will receive me."
—Psalm 27:10

THE CALAMITIES OF MISS CLEO

● ● ● ● ● ● ● ● ● ● ● ● ● ● ● ● ● ●

Remember when the Hula Hoop was all the rage? In mind-bending displays of dexterity, more than one smiling lass or laddy would wow an audience with the number of hoops they could spin at the same time. Today, they call that hoop-spinning "life in the corporate world." I guess the Hula Hoop is still around—at least Target has a peg with a bunch of hoops on it. They'd be perfect for folks my age. Hang a shower curtain on one of them, drape it over your body from the shoulders down, and walk across the beach without embarrassment during a vacation at the ocean.

Funny how the once-popular soon fades into society's sunset. It seems like only yesterday that "dial-a-future" was popular. An entrepreneurial miss named Cleo perfected a Jamaican slang and, for a price, told you about your past, present, and predictions over the telephone. She had trouble on the line in at least two areas: First, it was discovered that her Jamaican citizenship was as phony as a three-headed quarter. Miss Cleo was a native Californian. Second, she didn't predict a criminal investigation that discovered e-mails, infomercials, and phone pitches that were not intended to *enlighten* the listener, but rather to *lighten* them—to keep them on the line ringing up charges to her phone center.

Your future isn't that cloudy. It's as certain as the promise of God. If He says you have a hope, there isn't a network of naysayers in the world that can disconnect Him. These times may make you feel as uncertain as a Bingo player with double vision, but the fact is God's way is certain. It's not always clear, however. There are more twists than a Hula Hoop championship, and more false predictions than Miss Cleo's. But while you're lying awake, don't forget that God has already been to those places you're wondering about.

Extra Point
I will commit my times, as well as my time, to the Lord.

"There is surely a future hope for you,
and your hope will not be cut off."
—Proverbs 23:18

MORE PRIVILEGED THAN A PANDA

· · · · · · · · · · · · · · · · · · · ·

A leading newspaper filed suit to view the medical records of a panda at a national zoo, following its early demise. For months prior to its passing, the same panda had been viewed live on camera. A video cam recorded its every whine or wiggle, sneeze or snooze. The zoo director refused the request, saying the release of the medical records would violate the animal's privacy rights.

There are times when I wish I was as privileged as a panda. From overhead cameras that record my stops (or semi-stops) at red lights, to my entire financial history being accessed by everyone but me when my credit card is swiped, to a counter sales person suddenly saying "Do you still live at 133 Main Street?" when she calls up my account on a store cash register, sometimes I feel like I'm on "Jerry Cam." I have less privacy than a panda.

Where will it stop? Researchers from national chain bakeries burying tiny recorders in store-bought pies to sample my "Mmm's" and "Aah's"? Clothing manufacturers installing weight scales in exit ramps of interstate highways, so that I can be flagged down by stretch-waist-slacks salespersons at the next intersection?

Even though your privacy is invaded from all directions, you'll always be more privileged than a panda. When you confess your past, God puts your records so far away He can't even reach them. We've seen how the past indiscretions of some have grown like ugly weeds through the freshly sown grass of their lives. But grace is greater than the past. Once admitted, your spiritual history becomes eternally off-limits to all of hell's accusers. God covers it with the blood of the Worthy Lamb.

Extra Point
Today, I will resist the enemy's attempts to review my past.

"Remember not the sins of my youth and my
rebellious ways; according to your love
remember me, for you are good, O LORD."
—Psalm 25:7

DUCT TAPE

· · · · · · · · · · · · · · · · · · · ·

I went to the hardware store the other day to pick up supplies. Now for me, supplies from the hardware store usually consist of a video on installing plastic borders around the flower bed and a free bag of popcorn from the machine near the entrance door. After I grabbed my bag of popcorn, I moseyed over to the duct tape rack. It wasn't totally unfamiliar territory, since most everything I fix is finished off with duct tape anyhow. It was empty. All the ducts in a row were gone. And the bin that normally holds rolls of the gray gold was as empty as a dish of Hershey Kisses at a dieting seminar. I was told there was a run on cautionary supplies. Duct tape, flashlights, batteries, first-aid kits, and cassette tapes of the Lawrence Welk reunion shows were in great demand.

Duct tape is even being sold online at eBay—alongside die-cast Ford Falcon replicas and stainless steel plates celebrating the birth of America. Why the run on rolls of the sticky strands that make grown men weep when they try to unwind and apply them to broken whats-its without their bonding together? Fear. Some of it natural and some conveniently contrived.

Folks intent on turning our courage to cowardice have hollered "Duck!" And for the most part, we've collectively bowed our heads in subservience. We're taking direct hits to our head. Our terror-filled thoughts have become notches in some smiling terrorist's gun belt. I'm of the opinion that God's only Son rules over the events of time and eternity.

He taught that when biblical prophecy unwinds like a roll of duct tape, it's not a bad thing. It's a good thing. It simply means that the first strains of eternity's prelude are beginning to fill the airwaves over the earth. We don't know what tomorrow holds. But we do know that if it happens to be the very worst, then the beginning of the very best has dawned!

Extra Point

Today, I will fill my thoughts with the promises of the future instead of the pain of the present.

"Your kingdom is an everlasting kingdom,
and your dominion endures through all generations.
The Lord is faithful to all his promises and
loving toward all he has made."
—Psalm 145:13

SUNDAE MASSACRE

A while back, the food industry was stewing over dessert statistics. Soufflé sales had fallen. Pie purchases had been sliced. And ice cream revenues had turned cold. It was a sundae massacre! Some said they didn't have *time* for dessert. It's a travesty!

I cut my sweet tooth on Grandma Wilson's homemade doughnuts. Dough cut perfectly into circles of delight and lovingly placed in a frying pan filled with boiling oil. Minutes later they were rescued and thrown onto a sheet of powdered sugar. Healthy? Probably not. But she made them with sucryl, the father of artificial sweeteners, so she claimed they were good for you. I believed her. Grandma Wilson couldn't be cut off at the doughnut pass, though. She served a quarter piece of hot apple pie along with the doughnuts and asked you if you wanted whipped cream.

By the time you finished dessert, you were in sugar shock! Folks didn't just walk away from Grandma's dessert table—they leaped. They bounded out the door into the car, and bounced up and down as they drove 70 mph in a 25 mph zone. They were so filled with sugar that if a police officer would have stopped them, their eyes would have been dilated the size of doughnut holes!

Too busy for desserts? That's good news for the dieticians but its bad news for the fitness folks—and bad news for us. It's not just a food thing. When we don't have time for the *like-to*, we are left only with the *have-to*. When delight has surrendered solely to duty, we will be the unfortunate souls who have lost the war. There is something far more serious than eliminating hot chocolate; it's missing the cup of life. Jesus made sure His disciples didn't miss out. "Then, because so many people were coming and going that they did not even have a chance to eat, he said to them, 'Come with me by yourselves to a quiet place and get some rest'" (Mark 6:31).

Jesus didn't call a timeout so that His disciples could memorize another game plan. He wanted them to learn how much strength they would gain by a brief moment of doing nothing.

Extra Point
Today, I will give myself a timeout. I will shelve
a duty for the sake of a delight.

"Therefore my heart is glad and my tongue rejoices;
my body also will rest secure."
—Psalm 16:9

DR. ROBOT

● ● ● ● ● ● ● ● ● ● ● ● ● ● ● ● ● ● ● ●

ot only is a physician who makes house calls as rare as an electric funeral fan, new doctors may not even be in the same county when they remove your appendix. Robots are in medical training (in machine shops, I suppose) preparing to do surgical procedures. If you've ever met medical doctors that seemed to have ice in their veins, wait 'til you meet one that has 3-in-1 oil flowing through them!

Real live doctors are being trained to sit across the operating room at a control panel and manipulate the surgical "hands" of a robot through machine-made incisions. These combination camera, scalpel, and suture machines will probably change medicine forever, merging HMO and HBO!

What's next? Robotic control panels installed in golf carts linked to a satellite? Doctors able to operate during a game of golf, making a hole-in-one at approximately the same time they make a *hole-in-you*?

I've been to Dr. Robot—or at least it seemed like it. "What are we here for?" he asked blandly. I said, "I don't know what you're here for but I'm here because my back hurts!"

No answer. No smile. Dr. Robot didn't look up from his opened manila folder. He just gave me some exercises to do (running in place). "Will that help my arthritis?" I asked. Dr. Robot kept looking at the medical record and replied with all the pathos of a carburetor, "No, but the pain in your knees will take your mind off it. Here, take this invoice to the receptionist," he said as he left the room.

Some poor souls think of God as operating the universe from some celestial control panel, so far removed from the human condition that He can't feel a pulse, let alone pain. The truth is the God of the universe is well-versed in the problems of flesh and blood folks. He became one of them. God's grace is not just about power. It is also about proximity. He stepped from behind the farthest galaxy to stand alongside us in the midst of our deepest infirmity.

Extra Point
I will learn to understand that God understands!

"I have set the Lord always before me. Because he
is at my right hand, I will not be shaken."
—Psalm 16:8

$HADOW GOVERNMENT

called the county government offices the other day. First, I discovered that no one was working there. Whoever turned the coffee pot off for the night, before hurrying home to watch *Wheel of Fortune,* turned on a recorded message.

"Thank you for calling your friendly county government," the voice said. "If you would like the treasurer's office, please press 1. If you are calling any other department, please hang up now." I had assumed that my tax money was going to road improvements instead of the Missing Persons Bureau! I pressed 1. Surely there would be someone at the treasurer's office. A lonely custodian answered the phone, "Yeah?" Surprised at the answer, I said, "Could you please connect me to the building permit department?"

"It's eight-o-clock!" the custodian said.

"Perhaps you could help me," I implored. "I'm building a shed for some unused tools in my backyard and I'd like permission to hire someone else to build it."

"Go for it!" she replied, and hung up.

From time to time, your government really is missing. Officials are ordered to pack their lunch coolers and go to an underground bunker. It's then called a Shadow Government. If the worst-case happens, the wheels of bureaucracy will only hit a speed bump.

The Bible tells of another shadow government. Christian citizens of an unseen kingdom: A vast spiritual assembly that refuses to fear what happens. Supernatural-born citizens who's real and final home isn't within range of the bombs or bullets of evil. Whose King once was seen but now is unseen. Whose government operates in a hidden world above the layers of the earth—sending spiritual welfare checks, deploying angel troops to the battlefields of the soul, holding frail hands, and hearing faint prayers.

Extra Point
I will not be a captive to the headlines.

"You answer us with awesome deeds of righteousness,
O God our Savior, the hope of all the ends of the earth
and of the farthest seas, who formed the mountains
by your power, having armed yourself with strength,
who stilled the roaring of the seas, the roaring of
their waves, and the turmoil of the nations."
—Psalm 65:5–7

SHOPPING ONLINE

● ● ● ● ● ● ● ● ● ● ● ● ● ● ● ●

A trip to the Benjamin Franklin store used to be the highlight of the week. Now shopping online has taken its place. It's not only a way to spend leisure time, it's also a good way to keep your credit card in shape. An estimated fifty million people shop at one e-store alone. Fifty million buyers! Talk about a problem finding your car in the parking lot! The cyber-store is the brainchild of an engineer whose philosophy was to offer an Internet place where buying and selling in small increments would result in a larger blessing, both for him and for folks like the velvet Elvis painting collectors of the world.

Breathless anticipation fills the cyber room as the bidder makes an "e-offer," and then rushes to the kitchen for a grilled cheese sandwich and a glass of milk to relieve the stress of shopping and to kill time while a million other people make their move on the item in question. (Perhaps on an upright piano, which may be purchased for a song but will cost you more than your first semester in college for shipping.) One-upsmanship is the mark of a successful online shopper. One dollar more. One minute earlier. One product description better. One clearer picture—without a thumb over the digital camera lens.

I confess I'm not much into cyber-shopping. I like to squeeze the Charmin and make sure the head of lettuce bounces off the produce aisle floor before I make a purchase. Besides, how can you be sure that the Lexus automobile in the cyber-picture won't turn out to be a Volkswagen bus, once you've made the trip to Pittsburgh?

Incremental blessing isn't new. God is always raising the bid on His provisions. And He adds—or subtracts—according to our need. Every moment counts. Even the relaxing moments. God-blessed leisure is part of a God-blessed life. God modeled the pause. When He formed the worlds, He took time to rest from His labors. His strength was limitless but His wisdom taught us by example to cease and desist from time to time—for our sakes, and for the sake of those around us.

Extra Point
I will use leisure time to reflect on God's goodness.

"Be at rest once more, O my soul, for the
LORD has been good to you."
—Psalm 116:7

Voting Booth

● ● ● ● ● ● ● ● ● ● ● ● ● ● ● ● ●

During the elections, there are more political promises per TV hour than there are half shells in an oyster bar. And the political hopefuls are as agreeable as twin three-year-olds in the back seat of a compact car on a cross country vacation. Campaigns of the past give us an idea of what will happen. One politician hired professional models to represent his family on a campaign mailer. Thankfully, just before his kids turned themselves in to the foster care program, the picture on the mailer was changed. Had the cute and handsome edition been mailed, there would have been enough frost in the air at the candidate's house to chill the orange juice without refrigeration!

I respect the voting process; it's the voting that unnerves me. Having a severe technological disorder, I'm first intimidated by the voting machines. Row after row of buttons, lights, levers, artificial pens, and animal caricatures. I'm glad for those ugly curtains! Once inside the voting booth, I pull the curtain lever (helped by a precinct volunteer wearing donkey ears and an elephant nose) and start reading the instructions. I read every word, until I hear folks outside the curtain start to whistle Civil War songs. After as much angst

76

as a chad counter from Florida, I finally make my choice—
then go back over the instructions, word by word, to make
sure I voted for the right candidate. And the winner seldom
carries out the promises of his or her platform!

Now before you decide to pack citizenship papers and
move to another planet, remember that one vote will over-
ride every other: God's vote. His Yea or Nay still controls
the thermostat of the political climate. No one will rise to
the top without the prior approval of the One who sits above
every throne, dominion, or political district. And He'll
never be a lame duck. Whether you are on your first year of
AARP, or your last month of AAA, the solution to your
concerns is the same. You can weather the storm because
God is still at the helm.

Extra Point
What's happening isn't greater than Who's watching.

"All the ends of the earth will remember and
turn to the LORD, and all the families of the
nations will bow down before him."
—Psalm 22:27

Wi-Fi Wonders

● ● ● ● ● ● ● ● ● ● ● ● ● ● ● ● ● ●

They're everywhere. Coffee shops, fast food restaurants, book stores, hotel lobbies. People with laptop or handheld computers sitting at tiny tables with their herbal teas, coffee lattes, or bottled waters, searching the Internet for the best prices on air purifiers or denture cream. One Internet search engine alone dances around space and retrieves over 200 million sites each day.

I was born in the extension cord era. It didn't run if it wasn't plugged-in. From electric fans to portable black and white TV's with a vertical hold button so small you needed a magnifying glass to stop the ups and downs, being connected meant you were within range of a wall outlet. The real power was in the length of the cord. Now we're in the Wi-Fi era. The old connections are as obsolete as an adapter ring on a 45 rpm record of Connie Francis singing "Who's Sorry Now?" Wireless fidelity (Wi-Fi) has taken over. Now for someone like me, who had to take a night course to learn how to delete a sentence in a Word document without using a gum eraser on the computer screen, all of this is intimidating.

But I was intrigued by something one of the new Willy Wonka wireless guys said, "Google, combined with Wi-Fi, is a little bit like God. God is wireless. God is everywhere, and God sees and knows everything." Whoa! Sounds like an engineer on the Tower of Babel project, doesn't it? "Then they said, 'Come, let us build ourselves a city, with a tower that reaches to the heavens, so that we may make a name for ourselves and not be scattered over the face of the whole earth'" (Genesis 11:4).

Then the Building Inspector came for a look-see: "The Lord came down to see the city and the tower that the men were building" (v. 5). Even as He gave it the once-over, He knew that there wouldn't be a dedication ceremony. Technology still needs someone in charge—someone who won't be threatened by its bits and bytes, circuits and cells.

Extra Point
I will not fear technology. I will use it to
teach others about Christ.

"Say to wisdom, 'You are my sister,' and call
understanding your kinsman."
—Proverbs 7:4

PLASTIC TROPHY

O ne national pastime is watching celebrities take
potshots at their feet. Often it happens during
televised ceremonies that "honor" the acts or acting of
those whose ticket to the stars came from the frequent flyer
miles of fellow earthlings—folks like us who don't send limo
drivers to pick up our turkey subs at the deli.

Celebrity is a taxing situation. I know from experience. I
once won a horseshoe-throwing contest at a Sunday school
picnic. My whole life changed with a ringer that sent a
leaner to the showers. I stood in the middle of a vast crowd
of several and received my reward: a gold-painted, plastic
trophy, probably costing less than the price tag on a tooth-
pick. Somehow it was lost in one of many moves. Too bad!
My grandchildren would have loved to pass it around, taking turns displaying it on the mantels of their fireplaces.
Instead, some unworthy finder probably held it up and
bragged about winning the Kentucky Derby. Amazing how
some claim thrones when they should settle for folding
chairs.

That was the case for one celebrity who not only tripped on
the red carpet but took a self-inflicted shot to his metatarsal

bones. He abused his fifteen seconds of fame to spew venom about the leader of his country. I'm glad he had the opportunity. He has every right to use the "demo" in democracy. I just hope he didn't think he was speaking for all of us! The overwhelming majority breathe a silent prayer of thanksgiving that they live in a country where its leaders can say grace over meals in public, and invoke God's blessings on the comings and goings of its people.

That's a great hope for these days. Rest assured that kings or cultures will sit on thrones that have been built in the workshop of the heavens.

Extra Point
I will be more patient with those who express their freedoms in non-traditional ways, while still expressing mine.

"Nations are in uproar, kingdoms fall; he lifts his voice,
the earth melts. The LORD Almighty is with us;
the God of Jacob is our fortress."
—Psalm 46:6–7

TELEPHONE AD

. . . .

My cell phone rang. I was 500 miles from home. I had just talked with one daughter, and was sitting in a restaurant by the other. My wife had just removed her glasses, signaling the tabulation of the bill the waitress had just delivered to the table was complete. The phone's ring tone had just about finished the first measures of "Ode to Joy" when I noticed the little message light blinking. It had to be an urgent message! I nearly spilled a full glass of lemonade, broke my grandson's nose with an elbow, and pulled a muscle trying to raise the phone's antennae.

Sure enough, it was an urgent message: "Save $'s on your phone bill," it read. "WHO WAS IT?" the missus shouted, over the loud noise.

"IT WAS THE PHONE COMPANY," I shouted back.

"WHAT?" she again shouted over the restaurant music that was so loud it was shaking the salt and pepper bottles in their wrought iron holders.

"IT WAS AN AD!" I answered.

The missus shouted, "WELL, I'M MAD TOO! THEY SHOULD KNOW BETTER THAN TO CALL WHEN WE'RE VISITING OUR FAMILY!"

I looked at the urgent message. I had seen it before. It was in a letter from the cell phone provider. Evidently the company had hired a summer intern and she was as bored as a lifeguard at a lawn sprinkler convention. "I need something to *dooooo*," I could imagine her whine. "Okay," her supervisor must have said. "Take this letter and re-type it. Then send it electronically to all of our customers. One of those idiots will surely read it!"

Frankly, getting used to all these gadgets is as frustrating as trying to open a package of AA batteries. Paul the apostle must have been thinking about that when he sent the prototype of a text message to one of his students: Timothy. "Godliness with contentment is great gain" (1 Timothy 6:6).

Extra Point
I will learn how to adapt to the times
without abandoning the truth.

"Know that the LORD has set apart the godly for himself;
the LORD will hear when I call to him."
—Psalm 4:3

$HOPPIN(

hopping makes me tired. Put as many smiley faces on the mark-down signs as you please, you'll only cheer me for awhile. The rest is simply an endurance test. First, store managers don't know about the "if-it-ain't-broke-don't-fix-it" policy. They've eliminated the elevator music. Now, the only store sounds come from someone trying out a Galactic War computer game. I liked the canned music. It was fun trying to guess what song was playing. Later in life, I learned that there never was a song, only sampled recordings of corporate executives playing wax paper-covered pocket combs.

There are other things about shopping that tire me. I'm tired of people forcing shopping carts on me. My philosophy is if you've got a cart, you'll get a lot. I'd rather carry one of those plastic baskets. But store managers are smart. They don't hand out plastic baskets. They want you to fill shopping carts!

I'm also tired of check-out lines. Frankly, I've nearly "checked out" in some of them. Usually the only one with the light on is about a quarter-mile away. And by the time you've run to the light, it's gone out. The 12-year-old at the once-lit counter is taking a chewing gum break.

And sometimes, the store's sales associates tire me. "Do you have this shirt in my size," I ask the man pasting tags on toiletries in Aisle 9. He finally looks at me, and responds: "I'm not in clothes, mister, I'm in toiletries. Clothes are in aisle 47, next to Sporting Goods. And guessing your size, I think you'd better check out those pup tents while you're there."

It's a tiring process. You enter the store to buy more and leave with less. And an entire army of ambivalent store soldiers are waiting for an ambush! The tiresome trends of time may make you may feel as worn out as a brow-wiper at a weightlifting meet. God didn't promise freedom from exhaustion; He simply promised to strengthen you for the current battle.

Extra Point
Today I will let God's strength be the
source for my survival.

"A wise man has great power, and a man of
knowledge increases strength."
—Proverbs 24:5

WALKING BILLBOARD

andwich Signs seem to be as obsolete as lime green leisure suits and blue suede shoes. At the peak of their popularity, the familiar, hinged double sign advertised either the beginning of a new business or the end of the world. The walking billboards could be seen wandering along busy city streets, worn by folks with a smile or a frown—depending on the front and back copy.

The next generation sandwich sign lives! One TV network closed its evening news with a segment about a young woman who just had a web site tattooed to her forehead. "Oh yes," the news reporter commented. "It's permanent." For an advertising fee (that was hopefully enough to cover her tuition in a remedial wisdom class), the semi-attractive young woman will be wearing the dot com address through-out the rest of her life, or until she gets a good deal on sand-blasting.

Without the removal, she'll be easy to spot at the nursing home. "Susie?" the nursing supervisor will advise. "Sure! Just go down that hall, take a left at the bottled water machine and keep walking until you see a sad-faced woman holding her hand over her forehead. It's a tragic story.

When she was young, her fiancé convinced her to sell advertising space on her forehead so the couple could save enough money for a wedding trip to Omaha. She went to a trusted lady friend tattoo artist and had a dot com address permanently etched in her forehead. A month later, the dot com company went bankrupt, and her fiancé started dating the tattoo artist!"

The Bible says that those who have worn the name of Jesus on earth will be welcomed by Him to a place free of schemes and scams. In the mean time, display His name proudly—all day, every day. Of course those around you won't see it, other than in your compassion, your commitment, your confession, and your courage. Jesus didn't spend His time bragging about himself. He spent it serving others.

Extra Point
I will display Jesus in my life today by finding
something to do—for someone.

"One man gives freely, yet gains even more; another with-
holds unduly, but comes to poverty."
—Proverbs 11:24

CHURCH CHOIR

miss the choir. In many churches the choir robes are hanging in a storage closet behind the platform—along with the frayed bathrobes used by the Magi in the Christmas play, and a step-stool used by the amateur "actor" from a nearby church who plays Jesus during the ascension portion of the Easter drama. The conductor's baton is laying on the back of the keyboard, waiting the day the motor on the overhead screen malfunctions. In the event of such a lapse, the former president of the former choir will run to the platform, grab the baton, and jump straight into the air; spear the tiny hook on the screen, and manually pull it down, while the congregation waits for the words to the new song they've been singing every Sunday for the last few months.

It's a good time for a sing-along. Global disharmony has filled the airwaves with more static than a Louis Armstrong 45-rpm on a reconditioned Montgomery Ward record player with a bad needle. But very soon there'll be another sing-along. The date is yet to be announced, but I learned about the event as a child through the words of a gospel song: "When we all see Jesus, we'll sing and shout the victory." The first song of heaven will forever drown out the discord of earth.

In the mean time, all of us had better get in voice. Learn to sing harmony instead of always wanting the melody. Learn to acknowledge the honest praise of sincere folks who may not know all the songs we learned even before their vocal chords were formed. Besides, there won't be any golden oldies beyond the Gate. All the songs will be new and improved. So choir, enjoy the rest. You'll get your robe back on the other side. And you will be given an opportunity to sing new songs—songs of grace and glory in a land without discord.

Extra Point
No trend of the times will stop me from singing
praises in my heart to God.

"Great is the LORD, and most worthy of praise,
in the city of our God, his holy mountain."
—Psalm 48:1

PET COMMUNION

I had barely recovered from a news clip about forty-dollar sunglasses for Dobermans when I read a newspaper article about a communion service for Dachshunds and their friends. A church in Florida had added a contemporary worship service that included pets. I'm for most anything that gets people to church, but a pet communion service is one giant step out of my comfort zone.

I do remember a time when my Children's Church director had a conversation with the pastor following a disorderly Sunday morning. As she angrily gathered her paper and Velcro biblical characters from the flannel-graph board, she said rather boisterously, "I'm not working with those animals one more Sunday!!!" She nodded in our direction, but I didn't see any Dobermans or Dachshunds in the auditorium. Just regular kids and a smattering of us junior high boys who were making B-52 bombers out of the Sunday school lesson sheets.

The "pets in the pew" practice isn't new. Other religious persuasions have blessed pet turtles and such on the day nearest the birthday of St. Francis of Assisi. But I'll have to admit that pet communion is harder for me to swallow than a cactus cupcake.

It seems that I'm a little defensive about the Communion service. More than a ritual to me, it is a remembrance of Christ's Crucifixion—a time of reflection on the measures to which one person would go to save the life of another (1 Corinthians 11:25–26). Some have chosen on the spur of the moment to leap into flames to retrieve a trapped friend or loved one, and subsequently died from their injuries. But none, except the Savior, died for everyone. None have spent so much time pondering the significance of the sacrifice and then so willingly made it.

We are whole because He was willing to be torn. We are alive because He was willing to die. And we have hope because He was willing to endure hell to make us worthy of heaven.

Extra Point
I will use every sacred observance as fuel
for my service to others.

"I will sacrifice a thank offering to you and
call on the name of the LORD."
—Psalm 116:17

THANKS FOR THE MEMORIES

● ● ● ● ● ● ● ● ● ● ● ● ● ● ● ● ● ● ●

One by one, the stars of our past are fading away. Trigger is stuffed and on display in the Roy Rogers museum. Fury and Lassie have trotted into the sunset. And the Lone Ranger finally took off his mask. Another star, comedian Bob Hope, "played the last hole on the golf course of life." Only God knew his final score, but the galleys of people that watched him play out the more than three-score-and-ten rounds that were promised him, will be forever grateful. The evening newscaster reported that he had been singing "Thanks for the Memories."

Scores of grateful soldiers—Korea, Vietnam, and Gulf War veterans—were singing the same tune. They had seen Hope with his smirking smile and ski nose making them forget the moment by birthing a fresh memory in their hearts with an old joke. And they watched in wonder as compassion held court. Most were faceless comrades in crowds of military greens, whites, and blues who were given momentary significance by the celebrity making his seasonal sacrifices.

We can be a pleasant memory in someone's life. With a fix-up or repair, a spontaneous dinner invitation, a trip to the park, or a well-timed note or e-mail, we can make a permanent impression. Memories are far more than pages in a worn scrapbook or 5x7 pictures of once-skinny people on a mantle. They spring from a life that cares enough about others to execute "drive-by joy."

My father was funnier by accident than Bob Hope ever was on purpose. He could take the starch out of a prince with a story, a facial expression, or a song sung purposefully off-key. He never made a fortune—in fact, we had to borrow money for his funeral. But he left a treasure-chest full of pleasant memories to hundreds who smile even now at the mention of his name. He wasn't good at everything, but he was good at one thing: doing good. Good memories are born in good deeds.

Extra Point
I will make a fresh and pleasant memory in someone's life.

"He who pursues righteousness and love finds life,
prosperity and honor."
—Proverbs 21:21

LET SLEEPING SHIPS LIE

● ● ● ● ● ● ● ● ● ● ● ● ● ● ● ● ● ●

t sat regally on the dusty shelf of the antique store: a model sailing vessel. I had to search for it at first. Past three Tiffany lamp look-alikes, a bust of John F. Kennedy, and a half dozen RC Cola special edition bottles. I had to have it! A fan of the sea and sea vessels, I knew it would be the crowning jewel on my ship shelf. But once Tiffany, JFK, and RC were moved out of the way, I saw that the regal vessel had more than a few sea miles on it. The rigging was half gone, the crows nest looked like a condemned phone booth, and the anchor turned out to be a rusty safety pin. Even the captain was leaning over the railing, sick of the condition his once-beautiful ship was in! I decided to let sleeping ships lie.

I read that a salvage crew spent over six million dollars to raise the Monitor from its slumber off the coast of North Carolina. The iron-clad, steam-powered Civil War battleship took a dive—literally and figuratively—during an 1882 December storm as it was being towed to port. Salvagers raised portions of the once-mighty warrior's salty skeleton from the dismal depths.

What did they raise first? The gun turret. That's just what we need! Another rusty reminder of retribution! Granted, the twin cannons of the stately ship were probably the easiest to raise, but in the light (or dark, if you please) of world events, it might be better to leave those grudge symbols on the ocean floor.

It always is. Retribution is never seaworthy. Trying to get back at someone for something or other is as productive as trying to water ski behind the Titanic. God is more concerned with the better things of our future than the bitter things of our past. So let sleeping ships lie. If someone else wants to spend a fortune on salvaging the past rather than scanning the future, let them.

Extra Point
I will purposefully forget the hurtful deeds
of others and focus on their good.

"Fools mock at making amends for sin, but goodwill
is found among the upright. Each heart knows its own bitterness, and no one else can share its joy."
—Proverbs 14:9–10

ELECTIONS

● ● ● ● ● ● ● ● ● ● ● ● ● ● ● ● ●

f you're counting candidates for the next election, you probably have your shoes off by now. The list of White House, State House, or courthouse wannabes is longer than the list of names who must play on the roster of a parent-run little league team. If history is a factor, the contestants will range from pint-sized comedians to full-sized actresses.

I once served as a campaign manager for a class president candidate in a small high school. How small? The winner's victory party was held at McDonald's—in one booth. And I wasn't invited. My candidate finished one place behind first. I still don't understand it. We spent way over twenty dollars on poster board, blew up enough balloons to put a space shuttle in orbit, and promised to hire substitute exam-takers for athletes and cheerleaders. I even wrote the campaign speeches. One winning line said, "Ask not what you can do for your constituents; rather ask what your constituents can do for you!" And who can forget my campaign slogan: "If we don't win, at least we'll be glad we tried!"

One redeeming value of the election shenanigans is the process itself. I thank God for a nation whose constitution allows a choice among people and policies to form its philosophical fences! And I thank God for military bravehearts who put their life on the same line as their signatures, to certify the guarantee of that right.

But there are even more choices these days. Our very moral fabric is being frayed. Our children and grandchildren face a lion's den filled with godless tyrants who say that a country based on principle is as outmoded as a rotary dial telephone.

Others have chosen not to live by the whims and whines of secularists. Joshua lived in a biblical world that had a similar disregard for right and righteousness. But he was a father and grandfather who had courage enough to grab the hands of his family members and climb to the pinnacle of his times. And there, with a voice that echoed off the holy halls of heaven, he shouted his vote: "As for me and my household, we will serve the Lord" (Joshua 24:15).

Extra Point
I will make personal decisions based on how
they will influence those in my care.

"He who brings trouble on his family will inherit only wind, and the fool will be servant to the wise. The fruit of the righteous is a tree of life, and he who wins souls is wise."
—Proverbs 11:29–30

BEST DOG

· · · · · · · · · · · · · · · · · · ·

A noted comedian once had his pet serve as Best Dog at his wedding. Appropriately (or inappropriately) the cute canine wore a tux that matched the bridegroom's and heeled by his side during the ceremony. Having performed a hundred or more weddings over the years of my pastoral ministry, I've seen some "dogs" standing near the altar rail myself. But to the best of my knowledge, none of them had the blessing of the American Kennel Club.

Granted, the comedian's intent may have been truly sincere. Pity the bride that had to vie with a dog for the attention of the groom. If the pup's presence at the nuptials was a planned prank, then the groom should have taken another look at the vows. The ceremony that binds hearts in an earthly agreement under heaven's gaze deserves a little respect.

The loveliest bride I have ever seen once made promises to me that she has kept with stellar grace and ageless beauty. Promises kept through more sickness than health. Kept through more want than plenty. And kept with a love and cherish that all the poets of time could never write. At the front of a church packed with folks who didn't have enough corporate ingenuity to open a window on a sweltering summer day, the very best thing on earth happened to me: without a moment's hesitation, my bride said "I do."

That was just the beginning. The ceremony didn't make our marriage. A lifetime of putting each other first did. My bride and I knew that our times would be filled with laughter and tears, loss and gain, heartache and happiness. We were right. And the investment that each made to the relationship during those times resulted in the payoff.

It still pays—even after the anniversary silver is put away and we sprint (walk) toward the gold. If marriage is of God, then so are the principles that make it last. Selflessness is a family value that should never be abandoned.

Extra Point
I will add to my marriage—not subtract or divide.

"To do what is right and just is more acceptable
to the LORD than sacrifice."
—Proverbs 21:3

PROMISES

I don't remember my first kiss or my first half-truth. They both happened in my pre-teens. And both made me as nervous as a mosquito practicing touch and go landings on a bug zapper. My first kiss probably happened during church camp in the fifties. The idea was to choose a fair princess, sit with her during the church service, and then ask her for a walking date around the campgrounds afterwards. Hopefully before curfew there would be some serious hand-holding, a Dutch treat stop at the snack bar, and a quick kiss goodnight before either the camp nurse or the dorm counselor spotted the infraction.

My first half-truth probably preceded the kiss. I might have told the walk-ee that I would take her for a ride in the Chevy convertible that was promised upon my graduation from high school. The truth is I would inherit a '55 Buick sedan with the left front fender masked-taped to the car body and white "port-a-walls" on the tires that flapped like an ostrich trying to fly whenever the car exceeded forty miles-per-hour. I knew that because it belonged to my Uncle and he promised he would give it to me if I was lucky. I figured a goodnight kiss was about as lucky as I was going to get!

"Truth decay" is so prevalent that pretty soon it will have its own telethon. I once read that the average person tells two to three lies per day. Unfortunately the word *honest* often ends with a question mark rather than a period or an exclamation Point. We are a society that is prone to put mental asterisks beside the deeds or declarations of others. Hall of Fame achievement? Well, maybe. Original work? Well, who knows? We need promises with the assurance that their authors have uncrossed fingers. Promises that turn relationships into a living trust.

Not only is honesty the best policy, it's the best way to build a relationship with another human. Honesty that expresses its affection with conviction. Honesty that dares to say what it feels because it feels what it says.

Extra Point
I will build my relationships on the solid foundation of truth instead of the sinking sands of deception.

"A friend loves at all times, and a brother
is born for adversity."
—Proverbs 17:17

WEDDING DAY

alentines Day is one of the most popular days for weddings. Untold thousands of doe-eyed lovers will pay their "Do's" in churches, municipal buildings, gardens, and U-Rent wedding chapels. They'll stand before proper robed clergy, judges in jeans, or overweight Elvis impersonators in satin support garments. But none of those pompous or peculiar pairings can hold a candelabrum to one wedding: a darling pair of chickens were united in wholly "match-a-mony."

Chickens! You know, fowl folk that used to put a sparkle in Colonel Sander's eye. Someone had the brainy idea for an animal wedding; for chickens to waddle down the aisle, while a minimum wage organist tried to play "Here Comes the Bride" without changing the chord on her left hand or using any of the bass peddle notes. Chickens! I don't mean to suggest that they were afraid to get married. That's just who they were. The chick and chickadee were dressed in their finest, paraded before people who need to get a life, and pledged to love, honor, obey—and stay in the barnyard.

Chicken weddings? How silly! Love's sweet story knows no greater telling than the joining of human hands and hearts in the sacred quest for completeness we call a marriage. It is a time so sacred that angels must watch (and wish they had chosen the music). The same Creator who merged mountains and meadows, streams and seas, saw the incompleteness of one like me without my wife. On our wedding day, He added one plus one, and it equaled one.

In every marriage there eventually comes a time when you forget the words to the vows you once pledged. But time also proves that marriage goes beyond written words to an inner vow—a commitment to be as faithful and loving and tender in the latter years as you were in those first moments.

Extra Point

Today I will thank God for my spouse—living or deceased—and pledge to honor them by a life of compassion and caring.

"Love and faithfulness meet together; righteousness
and peace kiss each other."
—Psalm 85:10

TOY GUN SECURITY

"I think I hear a noise": the most dreaded words in any household. The minute that phrase falls from the lips of the missus, I know I'll be wandering the house like a member of the neighborhood council during a welcome party. When the noise warning sounds, I pick up an Oxford dictionary (tabletop edition) and begin the house roaming. If I encounter an intruder, I'll threaten to read the entire dictionary out loud. By the time I get to the G's, the intruder will probably call his colleagues and have them take our house off their hit list.

I read of one country's attempt to register its firearms and, in the process, discovered that a security guard in one of its major cities was carrying a toy gun to work. Granted, he was only one of thousands of private guards in the country but imagine if he was the one protecting *your* interests! "STOP OR I'LL CLICK!"

Come to think of it, we're all in the security business. We're guarding personal and family interests that are eternal in value. All enemy strongholds aren't in the mountains of some other country. There are some in your neighborhood. And the enemy doesn't always wear a camouflage uniform.

Sometimes he buys six-button suits at Saks Fifth Avenue. Sometimes he doesn't even carry a gun. Sometimes he carries a can't-lose stock option, or an erotic DVD, or a fitness center coupon that will take you away from home one more night of the week. Sometimes he even enlists volunteer soldiers to wage a war of words instead of bombs or bullets.

But faith in Christ puts you among heaven's elite commandos, and you're not armed with a water pistol (or a tabletop dictionary).

You go against intruders with more arms than NATO could ever inventory. You have Pentecost power not firepower. You're armed to the teeth with everything you need to make hell's troops wave white flags over your home and family.

The problem is, not everyone knows that. This is where you make your entrance. What you have learned by experience is what you need to teach the inexperienced.

Extra Point

I will find someone to mentor and equip
them for the good fight.

"Instruct a wise man and he will be wiser still; teach a
righteous man and he will add to his learning."
—Proverbs 9:9

Misinformation Minister

● ●

L aughter is good medicine, even if you have to down it in the crowded waiting room of a bunion specialist. Sometimes the serious sparks a funny. At the start of the Iraq war, we all were mesmerized by the updates from Iraq's then Information Minister. His claims that everything was calm in Baghdad were like the Shuffleboard Court Manager on the Titanic trying to sign up teams while lifeboat captains were hollering "All aboard!"

My favorite report was when the misinformed Minister reported from the roof of a luxury hotel that everything was under control — while trying to speak loud enough to drown out the sound of advancing tanks, flying jet fighters, and glancing bullets of Coalition forces. I never did see the assistant Information Minister but I surmised that he was crouched behind a barrel of crude oil a hundred-and-fifty yards away, purple-faced from trying not to burst out laughing!

I once tore ligaments in my knee during a football scrimmage. It wasn't as funny as the misinformation minister's reports. And neither was my attempt to walk on crutches for the very first time. My bride and I were living in a mobile home with tall wooden steps leading to the front door. The steps were the first thing I saw once I extricated myself from our Volkswagen Beetle. The trip from the hospital was challenging enough, trying to get comfortable in the front seat of a "Bug" while maneuvering a torn ligament and crutches. I knew the trip up the wooden steps to the mobile home door would be just as challenging. I was right. It would have been my finest moment if it hadn't of been for that tiny step up from the platform into the mobile home.

Picture crutches flying through the air, me laying face down in the entrance, and my dear wife (after asking if I was all right) laughing as if she were at a taping of the Red Skelton Show. It wasn't that humorous at the time, but looking back, it was one of the greatest "Funniest Home Video" moments of our lives. God paints some light strokes across the canvas of our lives, even when the background is dark.

Extra Point
I will learn how to laugh in spite of the load.

"A happy heart makes the face cheerful,
but heartache crushes the spirit."
—Proverbs 15:13

NO FRY ZONE

he "no fly zone" has a new friend: the "no *fry* zone." Take note, arteries. On guard, fat cells. You won't have fatty acids to kick around anymore! The trend in fast food fare is fruit and vegetables. Imagine your next drive-thru at the golden arches, and the voice in the little box says, "Would you like cauliflower with that?" The pressure's on the food industry. Someone's over-indulged and under-exercised child overdosed on French fries and Ronald took the fall.

Fresh from a court settlement, corporate chefs have devised a way to bring health back to the grease pits. Fruit cups. Veggies on a tray. An apple juice drink. And enough salad to feed a herd of marauding giraffes. Fast food eating will never be the same. Try dipping mandarin oranges in ketchup! Sharing an apple juice with your first date won't be the same as sipping on milk shakes. And try Super-sizing a grape!

The missus and I ordered one of the new salad entrees recently. It had all the taste of beach sandals! The oranges looked like they'd been in a tanning booth. The lettuce had an army camouflage look. And the low calorie dressing tasted like Freon from an air conditioner.

"I miss the old days," my lovely bride said.

"Me, too," I said mournfully. "Especially the fries." As tears of nostalgia welled in our bifocal-covered eyes, we drank our apple juice through straws and recited from memory the ice cream flavors at the old Howard Johnson restaurants.

So what's next? Will they take the coffee out of *CoffeeMate* or the pep out of *Pepsi*? Is less really better than more? I don't know about the potato pollution controversy but I do know that less is better in a lot of ways: Reduced worries. Reduced anger. Reduced introspection. Reduced discontent. Reduced selfishness. Come to think of it, there are a lot of fatty acids that clog our spiritual arteries. The heart we save may be our own.

Extra Point

Today, I will get rid of those things that
clog my spiritual arteries.

"Wash away all my iniquity and cleanse
me from my sin."
—Psalm 51:2

COOKING SUPPER

· · · · · · · · · · · · · · · · · ·

W hen the missus and I were first married, I decided
to cook supper. She was working in a clothing store
and I was a full-time, fifty-dollar-a-week associate
pastor of a church in a nearby city. We needed the extra
income, and I needed to learn how to cook. "I'll fix the meal,"
I said to my lovely bride on the phone. "Are you still there?"
I said after the long silence. A slight "Okay" soon traveled the
phone lines between the clothing store and our 12x55-foot
mobile home.

The minute she hung up I knew I was in trouble. I didn't
have a clue where to begin. I gathered enough pots and pans
to feed the Mormon Tabernacle Choir for an entire road
tour, took four pork chops from the freezer, leftover mashed
potatoes from the frig, opened a can of corn and started
"cooking."

The vegetable was next. I took a butter knife and a hammer,
and pounded the can of corn all around the lid. Eventually
I made enough of an opening to dribble the kernels into a
frying pan and poured some cooking oil on them. Matching
Hostess Twinkies would be dessert.

The table was set with our finest grocery-store-give-away flatware and a variety of plates and saucers. I even remembered to roll the "silverware" in a paper dinner napkin (which was easier than trying to remember how to set the table). I put the frozen pork chops in the broiler, the corn in the frying pan, the potatoes in a pot, the Twinkies on a saucer, and jumped in the car for the twenty-minute drive to pick my bride up from work.

In case anyone ever asks, it's not advisable to leave pork chops in the broiler for forty minutes! Opening the door upon our return to the mobile home looked like a re-make of the movie "Backdraft"! Later my bride and I had a romantic dinner at Burger Chef.

I'm glad that God has given us a recipe book: the Bible. There in verse and chapter appetizers or entrees of entire books, we have enough instruction to feed our faith until it seems almost full.

Extra Point
Today, I will be nourished by the Word.

"Your promises have been thoroughly tested,
and your servant loves them."
—Psalm 119:140

TRANSGENICS

W e knew it was coming. Genetic engineering has been on the burners of scientific and theological thought for some time ("Hello Dolly!"). Now for act two: transgenics. The lab coat folks have come up with a new way to raise the collective eyebrows of a society bored with reality TV by genetically engineering plants to speed their growth and make them resistant to things, like new subdivisions.

It would be enough to make George Orwell buy over-the-counter nerve pills. Imagine a world of corn that could be *sky*-high by the fourth of July or butter beans the size of New Hampshire. Science is not only out of the box; it has jumped the fence. It gives me the heebie-jeebies.

I've tried animal science. I wasn't cut out for that, either. I once thought of raising Dachshunds. I tried to give Heidi, our first dachshund, a pill for her allergies. If I remember right, she was allergic to two things: newspapers on the floor and going outside when it was raining. Getting the allergy pill down the reluctant and regurgitating throat of that wiener dog proved the theory that you *can* take one pill three times a day. Poor thing! All I could think about was getting checked for strep throat. Just the sight of a tongue depressor makes me gag! I could only imagine how the poor dog felt while I was force-feeding that pill down her throat—and just about ready to use a plunger to finish the project. Needless to say, I'm not ready to enter the field of transgenics.

But God did put a growth gene in the spiritual makeup of every believer. The very life of Christ has been injected by faith into the system of those who have trusted Him. So when you're about to launch that second (or third or fourth) career, don't be intimidated by it. God has provided all the necessary resources.

Extra Point
Today, I will mark my growth by how
much I am growing like Christ.

"May the favor of the Lord our God rest upon us;
establish the work of our hands for us—
yes, establish the work of our hands."
—Psalm 90:17

NOT-SO-FRIENDLY SKIES

● ● ● ● ● ● ● ● ● ● ● ● ● ● ● ● ● ●

To me, commercial flights are about as much fun as having my adenoids removed without an anesthetic— by a podiatrist. I try to be sympathetic with those airlines that have buckled their seatbelts during the turbulence of the times. Their motives are probably good. From Orville and Wilbur on, there has been a dedicated group that has prided itself in getting us from Point A to Point B without deploying those yellow masks from the cabin ceiling or causing us to use our seat cushions as life preservers. And you have to sympathize with those flight attendants who spent all that time in training memorizing those pre-flight instructions; only to have them ignored during their entire career. (I've had the same feeling when I've given the morning message in church!)

In one sense, the industry's load is lighter. They no longer have to worry about spilling hot food on passengers during in-flight lunches, or about the presence of anyone's luggage in the baggage claim area following touchdown.

Whether you're in coach or first class, concern is creeping in like sea gulls with a bad sense of direction. For some, the

"Security" in Social Security is beginning to be spelled with a small "s." Medical costs are rising faster than an Irish tenor on helium gas. From weather, to welfare, to warfare, the skies have turned decidedly unfriendly. But that doesn't mean they're out of control. The planet's Pilot is still at the wheel.

The Creator is still the Keeper. And the Keeper is still watching over the kept. Nothing will happen here that has not first been approved there.

Career change or retirement can be as scary as riding on the wing of an airplane—in flight. It's all new, there doesn't seem to be anything holding you up, and you'll probably experience some turbulence! But the One who rides the heavens still controls the altitude. And if you'll let Him, He'll take care of your attitude as well.

Extra Point
I will not let the world form my opinion
about my current condition.

"I was appointed from eternity, from the beginning, before
the world began. When there were no
oceans, I was given birth, when there were
no springs abounding with water."
—Proverbs 8:23–24

DIRECTIONS

● ● ● ● ● ● ● ● ● ● ● ● ● ● ● ● ● ● ●

My sister was listed in "Who's Who in Education." I think she listed me as one of her research projects. Direction was my problem. It wasn't about focus. It was about finding my way. I have a bad sense of direction. I could ask twelve people how to get to the post office and not remember a single turn. I'd have to follow a postal delivery truck until the driver finished her shift.

My wedding day was no exception. Since I had made the trip from the tiny side room by the church's platform to the front of the altar without getting lost, my bride probably assumed that I knew how I got there. What she didn't know was that during the pre-game talk in that "locker room," I wasn't rehearsing my vows. I was asking the preacher, the Best Man, the ushers, and the ring bearer for directions to the front of the church. The ring bearer looked straight up into my eyes and said, "I'm only going to tell you this one more time! You go out that door, take a right at the piano, and head toward that first line marked with masking tape!"

"Which side of the piano?" I asked nervously. "The side with the black and white keys?" The boy didn't respond. I panicked. If I hadn't been following the preacher out the door, I might have ended up in the church basement during the nuptials (or on top of the piano!).

The middle ages often demand a move: A relocation after retirement or career change. A condo instead of a large home. A smaller home because of an empty nest. Leaving the old and settling into the new can be as frustrating as trying to open a package of soup crackers at a restaurant. But God knows about your comings and goings. He walked you through the first stages of your life, and He won't leave you now.

Extra Point
I will trust the Lord for every curve in the road of my life.

"Even though I walk through the valley of the shadow of
death, I will fear no evil, for you are with me;
your rod and your staff, they comfort me."
—Psalm 23:4

ALL THUMBS

'm learning to use the new generation of handheld computers and cell phones. It hasn't been easy. It seems like only yesterday I was pounding on one of those oversized Remington typewriters, trying to convince an English teacher that I could spell "English" with just one "n"—and worrying that I would break my knuckles in the process. The tiny keyboards on the new gizmos are challenging, to say the least. The first time I tried to send a text message, I typed out the Greek word for Czechoslovakia. I admit it; I'm all thumbs when it comes to the new messaging machinery. But being all thumbs is also a good thing. Nowadays, the index finger is only used to signal the number of Grande coffees at the drive-up window or count the chronological age of very young children. It isn't even used in parenting anymore!

Those under the age of a Social Security recipient and above the age of a pre-school dropout now use their thumbs for dialing cell phone numbers. That explains why an obviously upset Generation X airline passenger kept calling our home well into the night, asking for baggage claim. After the third call, I should have said, "Go outside and stand by the curb. We'll have your luggage there within the next twenty minutes!"

Those thumb researchers aren't the first to try to re-define our strengths. Some of us have been characterized as being "all thumbs" even when we weren't text-messaging. The bottom line: Don't let anyone but your Creator judge your abilities—especially because of your age. You are not superior or inferior because you can or cannot speed-dial a pizza delivery with the same digit you used to hitchhike to Milwaukee. Your authenticity—rather than your dexterity—defines your strength. God created you from the inside out. And He has given you dexterity enough to hold His hand even when others are pointing their fingers at you.

Extra Point
I know what I can do is as good, or better, than anyone else. And I'll do it for God's glory.

"For you created my inmost being; you knit me
together in my mother's womb. I praise you
because I am fearfully and wonderfully made;
your works are wonderful, I know that full well."
—Psalm 139:13–14

No-Duty Guard Duty

● ● ● ● ● ● ● ● ● ● ● ● ● ● ● ● ● ● ●

When I was in pre-primary, I retrieved some tomatoes from a neighbor's garden—without the appropriate permission. Back then it was called stealing. Today it might be called a trans-ethical deployment of produce. The whole incident came to an embarrassing conclusion. Namely, I had to hold my father's hand in one of those confessional parades, down the sidewalk, across the street, and up the porch steps of you-know-who. There was a sudden knocking. I couldn't tell whether it was the door or my knees. When the neighbor opened the door and lumbered onto the porch, my father said, "Jerry has something he wants to tell you." A second commandment was broken: Bearing false witness! I didn't want to tell that neighbor anything! The tomato caper was over. I was trapped like a pickpocket at a Velcro convention.

When I read about it, I knew how the culprit who stole the Crucifixion felt. No, not the real one; the surreal one. Some prison guards took an original Salvador Dali painting of the Crucifixion from the wall of a "high security jail" in a major metropolitan city. Pity the judge! It would be tough to lower the gavel on someone who parks in your same parking lot. But justice had to be served to the no-duty guards. They had substituted a fake Dali. And it would be confusing to have a mere copy hanging in the jail hallway.

Thankfully, the real Crucifixion is in its rightful place: in history and in our hearts. It can't be copied. No replicas there. No other event in time was so genuine—so unique.

He took the lead. The Leader expressed leadership in a way that a thousand authors could never express. The very Son of God allowed Himself to be nailed to the tree that bore our initials on its rough surface. Leading by laying His life on the line. Tired. In pain. Forsaken by those who once looked up to Him. He showed all of us how to lead when the leading gets tough.

Extra Point
I will seek a place of Christ-filled leadership
and lead like Christ.

"Since you are my rock and my fortress, for the
sake of your name lead and guide me."
—Psalm 31:3

THE LAYOFF

I was paid $1.15 per hour on my first job. Today, the time cards would cost more than that. One day I asked for a raise. My boss looked as if he had just sat on the pointed end of a javelin. "Raise?" he began, "When I was your age I had to walk two miles to my school." (He was busy and didn't realize he was giving the wrong speech!)

That didn't help my financial condition. If I were offered free packets of sugar from the work break room, I would have had to make payments on them. And soon the good news came, "We're cutting back," Diamond Jim (my boss) said with a somber look, "I'm afraid I'll have to lay you off."

I replied lightly, "I'm afraid of that, too." It didn't work. So I gathered all my used sack lunch bags and went out into the cold August day. *Where would I ever make that kind of money again?* I wondered.

The children of Israel understood stressful financial times. The enemy was stalking them like a hungry ninth-grader standing over a plate full of fresh chocolate chip cookies. Their reaction, "It would have been better for us to serve the Egyptians than to die in the desert!" (Exodus 14:12). Obviously, they forgot two things. First, they forgot who was for them. Moses reminded them, "The Lord will fight for you; you need only to be still" (Exodus 14:14). They didn't need another finance committee meeting; they needed a "fully committed meeting." The Chief Financial Officer of the Eternal Kingdom was working on the budget—and it would include everything they needed, just when they needed it most.

Second, they forgot how to trust Him. Quiet faith was the answer: "You need only to be still." Worrying, whining, or wishing wasn't the answer. It isn't your answer, either. God has the third shift. He'll be awake tonight, weaving His perfect will through the threads of your life.

Think about it. God has situated himself in your situation. The savings and loan of heaven isn't threatened by dancing Dow Jones' averages; and the "Kingdom Reserve Board" won't need to raise or lower percentages to stimulate God's economy.

Extra Point
I'll write down my greatest need, take it to God
in prayer, and then say, "Father, I believe that you
are working this out for my good."

"Wealth and riches are in his house, and his
righteousness endures forever."
—Psalm 112:3

THREE-YEAR-OLD FOOD

he "Spicy Beef" sandwich always looks good in the picture—especially on the clip-out coupon. But after fifty-plus years of forays into the restaurant chains of the universe, I've learned that the camera may "never lie" but it can stretch the truth farther than suspenders on a rhinoceros with stomach bloating. Some of those pictured edibles can be totally unpalatable. For example, once the "fresh" garden salad pictured on the overhead menu passes over the counter, the leaves look older than Adam & Eve's first Sunday-go-to-meetin' clothes. I once ordered a hamburger that looked as if it were piled with beef, tomatoes, onions, lettuce—and probably some special sauce. Once the counter person handed it to me on a plastic tray, it looked as if the entire rush hour traffic of Los Angeles had run over it.

I'm told that the government has meals that will last longer. (Too bad they can't make a dollar go farther!) MREs (Meals Ready To Eat) have been developed so that soldiers—and husbands whose wives attend women's conventions in large auditoriums—can keep them for up to three years if necessary.

Now I know from my own experience that breath mints have at least a ten-year life expectancy, since I've retrieved them from the side pockets of blue suits just as the AmVets truck rolled into the driveway. And I've tasted fruitcake that surely must have been created in the galley of Christopher Columbus' cruise ship. So, it's possible for the government to make three-year-old food. If the technology continues to advance, cheese sandwiches may soon last longer than prehistoric pizzas.

I doubt that many of us would serve three-year-old sandwiches to our guests. But what about the offerings we serve the Lord. He deserves the freshest morsels of our time, our talent, and our treasure. Our gifts really should reflect what's on the menu of our heart.

Extra Point

I will be a wise steward-manager of his resources.

"The sluggard's craving will be the death of him, because his hands refuse to work. All day long he craves for more, but the righteous give without sparing."
—Proverbs 21:25–26

PRINCE OF PATCHWORK

● ● ● ● ● ● ● ● ● ● ● ● ● ● ● ● ● ● ● ●

For those who are responsible for the upkeep of yours or someone else's property, remember this: Duct tape is the Prince of Patchwork, and we are its loyal subjects. Anyone who has ever tried to tame the inches-wide answer to earth's crevices or cracks knows it's domain. Take your eyes off a mere slip of some of the glued fabric for nanoseconds, and it will curl up like an Olympic diver doing a double what's-it. Or, it will rush back to its rolled home quicker than a cheap measuring tape and bury itself in a field of gray, daring you to find its pouting lip to start the unraveling process all over again.

Duct tape can patch just about everything. I've seen it on car fenders, chair legs, skirt hems, furniture fabric, shoe soles, hat brims, and dog collars.

In case the medical field is stuck on the material, I'm checking the hospital bill after my surgeries to make sure I'm not being held together by duct tape. I can only imagine what a day in the sun would do to a gallbladder incision once the tape began to un-stick!

Who knows what other segments of our society are secretly pledging their loyalty to the Prince of Patchwork. Does duct tape have a secret Wall Street listing—and is our economy being held together underneath its surface? I simply don't know. So mechanically challenged that I would need an instructional video just to change the air in my car tires, I'm a duct tape fan.

Duct tape may be the earthly Prince of Patchwork, but it's not a substitute for the hold-all, help-all power and promises of the Christ. He is the solitary answer for these broken times. He holds your world together, first, by holding you. If it hasn't happened yet, it will. In the home, on the job, at work, or at play, something or someone will come unglued. It's simply a fact of life. When it happens, remember that the King of Glory is greater than the Prince of Patchwork. Human means are no match for heavenly mercy!

Extra Point
Grace is the glue that binds us to heaven.

"You answer us with awesome deeds of righteousness, O God our Savior, the hope of all the ends of the earth and of the farthest seas."
—Psalm 65:5